T0269944

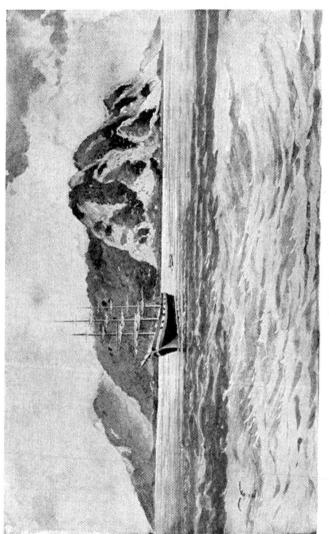

PITCAIRN ISLAND.

Mutiny of the Bounty

and

Story of Pitcairn Island

1790—1894

———

By

Rosalind Amelia Young

A Native Daughter

———

University Press of the Pacific
Honolulu, Hawaii

Mutiny of the Bounty and Story of Pitcairn Island
1790 - 1894

by
Rosalind Amelia Young

ISBN: 1-4102-0846-X

University Press of the Pacific
Honolulu, Hawaii
http://www.universitypressofthepacific.com

TO

CLARA FREEMAN CROCKER,

LAURA P. WHITE,

And to the many dear friends who have ever shown

an interest in the history of Pitcairn

Island, this little work is

AFFECTIONATELY DEDICATED

by the Author.

INTRODUCTION.

MANY books have been written on the history of Pitcairn Island, while magazine articles and newspaper sketches almost without number have appeared from time to time, treating on some feature of the island or its history. While there are some points of disagreement between the different writers, they have in the main given a fairly good history of the island, and of its condition many years ago, though some of their statements have been somewhat exaggerated. That it is inevitable that some errors should creep into such histories may be clearly seen from the fact that very few of the writers have ever visited the island, while those who have done so, remained but a short time, and so could see but one side of life on that isolated spot.

The present work is written by a native of the island, and one who has practically spent her whole life on the island, a few years of her childhood only having been spent on Norfolk Island. While her lifetime does not cover quite one-half of the time covered by the history of the island, she had access for many years to one at least who remembered events that occurred before the beginning of the present century. The author's father was the second oldest man of the community at the time of his death, in September, 1893, and was a grandson of John Adams, one of the mutineers of the *Bounty*, whose death took place in 1829. She has thus had the best of advantages for obtaining a correct knowledge of the island history.

The writer of this introduction spent over eighteen months on the island, leaving there February 9 of the present year, and, as far as his observation goes, believes that the statements contained in this book are strictly reliable.

The island, though but a dot on the broad Pacific, being but two and one-quarter miles long by one and a half miles wide, is an interesting spot, and its history reads like a romance. Its location is a favorable one, being about two degrees south of the tropic of Capricorn, for which reason the weather is never so intensely hot as in some of the islands of the south seas, and is never cold. Beautiful tropical trees,—the tall, graceful cocoanut palm, the wide-spreading banyan, the pandanus palm, and others,—cover its surface from end to end. Refreshing breezes, cooled and moistened by passing over thousands of miles of ocean, constantly fan the surface of this lovely isle. It can be truthfully said of this island that

" Every prospect pleases."

The people who inhabit this little Eden are half castes, their dark features and black hair plainly betraying their Tahitian blood, though some of them have quite light complexion and blue eyes. At present there are but about one hundred and thirty of the inhabitants. The kindness and hospitality of this interesting people have been remarked by all who have ever called at the island.

We believe this little book will be read with profit and delight by all who are so fortunate as to secure a copy.

E. H. GATES.

S'. Helena, Cal., July 30, 1894.

CONTENTS.

CONTENTS.

CHAPTER XX.

CHAPTER XXI.

CHAPTER XXII.

CHAPTER XXIII.

ILLUSTRATIONS.

CHAPTER I.

OWARD the close of the eight-eenth century, at a time when events producing the most important results were occur-ring among some of the nations of the earth, there was being laid, unconsciously, the foundation of a history which in all its points could equal, if not surpass, any tale of fiction.

During the reign of King George Third, of England, the English Government considered it advisable to introduce, if possible, the breadfruit into her colonies in the West Indies, and for this purpose a ship was specially fitted out and provisioned. A small sloop-of-war, named the *Bounty*, was the one provided, and her internal arrangements were begun and completed with the view of transferring, with the least possible injury, the tender plants from their native soil.

On the twenty-ninth day of December, 1787, the *Bounty* left England, under orders to proceed to the Society Islands, for the purpose of procuring plants of

the breadfruit tree, to be conveyed to the West Indies.
Lieutenant William Bligh was appointed commander,
and about forty-five persons, including a gardener,
made up the crew. Provisions for eighteen months
were put on board.

The different feelings that possessed the minds of
the men who were leaving behind them what they held
most sacred and dear on earth, may be imagined; yet
were they doubtless cheered by the thought of one
day meeting again the dear friends at home, when the
long separation was ended. But for the ship, and for
some of the crew, it was never to be, and could the
results of that voyage have been foreseen, it is a question how many of those who then left their native land
would have dared to embark on a journey that was to
be fraught with events so startling in their nature, and
that was to end so strangely, that even at this distant
day the story is repeated and listened to with sustained
interest, not only by strangers, but by the immediate
descendants of the misguided men, who themselves fell
victims at last to their own wrongdoing.

The voyage out was safely accomplished, the *Bounty*
having arrived at Tahiti in the month of October,
the year following her departure from England. Six
months were spent at the island collecting and stowing
away the plants, the crew in the meanwhile becoming
very friendly with the natives. A violent storm threatening, Captain Bligh deemed it prudent to leave. This
was in April, 1789.

Leaving Tahiti, the *Bounty* went on to Anamooka,

where Captain Bligh took in water, fruits, goats, and
other live stock, and put to sea again on the 26th of
the same month.   It was after leaving the last mentioned island that some dissatisfaction was first noticed
among the crew.   Hitherto, if there had been cause
for complaint respecting the captain's treatment of
those he commanded, it had not been openly manifested.   It has now become matter of history that
William Bligh possessed a tyrannical temper, and frequently had misunderstandings with his officers and
men.   This, and the fact that many of the crew had
formed intimate acquaintance with the people of the
islands, doubtless caused them to conceive the plan of
seizing the ship, after having disposed of the officers.

Shortly before the mutiny broke out, one of the
men, Fletcher Christian (master's mate), incurred the
captain's severe displeasure.   It is said that through
the advice of a young officer who perished in the *Pandora*, Christian first formed the design of mutiny, which
was so effectually carried out.   Be that as it may, the
night of the 28th of April, 1789, witnessed the out-
break on board the *Bounty*, as the mutinous crew rose
in arms against their captain.   Fletcher Christian,
aided by three other men, secured the person of Captain Bligh.   They entered his cabin, and dragged him
from his bed.   Being soon overpowered, his hands
were pinioned behind him, thus rendering him helpless
in the hands of his captors.

A boat had been made ready to receive the unfortunate Bligh and those of his companions who were to

share his fate, but the share of provisions allowed them was very small. Owing to the smallness of the size of the boat, only eighteen men besides the captain ventured to trust their lives in it. Others would gladly have accompanied the eighteen, but there was no possibility of obtaining room in the boat, already too full, and their only alternative was to remain in the ship with their misguided companions. The boat containing the unfortunate men being cut adrift was soon headed for the island of Tofoa, about thirty miles distant, where a landing was effected. The natives there showed a decidedly hostile spirit, and when made aware of the presence of the white men, they rushed down to the beach, shooting arrows and hurling stones at the intruders. A man named John Norton was killed. The other eighteen hastened to get beyond the reach of their pursuers and their arrows. Then commenced a voyage attended with so much hardship and misery in the exposed condition of the voyagers that even to this day it commands the admiration and excites the wonder of all who hear. Going over the vast distance of upwards of twelve hundred leagues, encountering every kind of weather, enduring dreadful sufferings, hunger, and thirst, these men at last reached the island of Timor, where was a Dutch settlement. Here they were shown the greatest hospitality and kindness by the governor. Leaving Timor, they went to Batavia, where Bligh and some of his officers took passage on a vessel bound for Europe. They eventually reached England in safety.

MOORLAND CLOSE, CUMBERLAND, THE BIRTHPLACE OF FLETCHER CHRISTIAN.

No time was lost in acquainting the English Government with the disastrous failure of the *Bounty's* mission, and, although there were some among the crew who, at the time of the mutiny, pleaded that no blame should be attached to them, the result showed that Bligh did not spare those whose hearts and hands were alike innocent of any wrong against him.   Very soon the *Pandora*, commanded by Captain Edwards, a man devoid of the humane feelings of kindness and pity, was sent in search of the men who had so willfully forgotten their duty.   Of these only fourteen were found, eight having accompanied Fletcher Christian, with the *Bounty*, and two of their number having been killed by the natives of Tahiti some little while before. These poor men were conveyed in irons on board the *Pandora*, where they were placed in a close room, with one small opening to admit light and air.   Chained to the floor, exposed to the most cruel treatment that the mind of the inhuman Edwards could conceive, enduring the heaviest privations, and compelled to live in their noisome den from day to day without any means of having it cleansed, the condition of these sufferers can more readily be imagined than described.

In this cruel position they were forced to exist; and when at last the *Pandora* was wrecked on a coral reef, the unfeeling Edwards would not listen to the piteous pleadings of the prisoners and release them, even to afford what help they might be able to render in trying to save the ship.   One sailor, however, possessed of humane feelings, would not willingly let so many of his fellow-creatures perish thus before his eyes, and, exerting all his strength, succeeded in accomplishing their release, but not until four of them had perished. On board the ship that finally conveyed them to England, they were treated as human beings, and allowed freedom from their chains. Of these ten men "four were acquitted; one was discharged on account of an informality in the indictment; the other five were found guilty and were condemned to death. Of these two received a pardon, and the three others were executed at Spithead," from which place they had sailed on their eventful voyage four years before.

THE ARRIVAL AT PITCAIRN

CHAPTER II.

DURING all this time where were Christian and the other guilty men who followed him? After having set the boat containing Bligh and his companions adrift, Fletcher Christian assumed command of the *Bounty*, and returned toward Tahiti. The ship was taken first to Toobonai, the intention of the men being to settle there; but, finding the place destitute of animals, they went to Tahiti to procure a stock of pigs and goats. Obtaining what they needed, they returned again to Toobouai, but found the natives hostile to their landing. Once more, and for the third and last time, the *Bounty* was brought to Tahiti, where she was anchored in Matavai Bay, on the 20th of September, 1789. Sixteen of the crew here landed, taking with them their share of the arms and other articles on board the *Bounty*. These were the men, it will be understood, who were discovered and taken away by the *Pandora*, as related in the previous chapter.

Leaving at Tahiti that portion of the crew whose choice it was to remain, Christian, accompanied by eight of his shipmates who decided to cast in their lot with him, sailed away from Tahiti forever. But this number was not all, for six of the native men, and ten women, and a girl of fifteen, were taken on board as wives and servants, the sailors having determined to seek some place where they could live secure from the danger of discovery. It is said that Christian, having seen an account of the discovery of a lone island in the Pacific Ocean, by Captain Cartaret, in the year 1767. directed the course of the ship to that place. It was named Pitcairn Island, after the young man who descried it, he being, as the story goes, a son of the Major Pitcairn who fell in the Battle of Bunker Hill.

On the twenty-third day of January, 1790, the *Bounty* reached her destination. The island, though small, being about five miles in circumference, and scarcely more than two miles across at its widest point, was thickly covered with a luxuriant growth of trees.

On coming near enough for a boat to venture, a small party went on shore to search the land. They effected a landing on the west side of the island, but, finding that a few yards from the sea the rocks rose perpendicularly to a forbidding height, and thinking to find a more convenient place for a settlement, they brought the ship round to the northeast side of the island. Here they managed to bring their boat safely to the shore, through perilous rocks and breakers. It did not take long to discover that the island had been,

and perhaps still was, inhabited, and fears were entertained lest they should be attacked by hostile natives.
Traces of former habitations,—*marais*, stone images,
rude pictures cut in the rocks, stone hatchets, etc., etc.,
—were evident proofs that human beings had once
lived on the island, and in addition to these, several
human skulls and other bones were afterward seen.

As day after day passed, and no one appeared to
molest them, the mutineers began to feel more secure
and safe, and preparations were made for a permanent
settlement. Their supply of water, though not abundant, was sufficient for their requirements, and the plants
brought with them from Tahiti would, in due course
of time, be able to supply their every want. But, first,
all trace of the ship must be destroyed. She was
driven near enough to the shore to allow of her being
fastened to a tree by means of a rope. Everything
that could be of service to the settlers was removed.
For greater safety, one little child was brought ashore
in a barrel, as the landing place for boats was very dangerous. When all had been removed from the ship,
she was set on fire, and destroyed.

There were those among the mutineers, if not all,
who were grieved that they should be obliged to
destroy the vessel that had been their home so long.
Especially was it so with John Mills, if his daughter's
testimony is correct, for she never wearied of telling
how her father sorrowed over the destruction of the
Bounty, as it was his hope one day to return in her to
England, even at the risk of his life. These fugitives

from justice spent the early days of their settlement
on Pitcairn Island in caves, and tents made of canvas,
while their cottages were being built.   Here, on this
solitary, uninhabited spot, Christian could, at least,
hope to hide himself and his guilty associates from
the extreme penalty of the law.

But no degree of outward security could bring peace
to a mind constantly disturbed with self-accusing
thoughts, or still the reproaches of a conscience
burdened with guilt and remorse.   Poor, misguided
men!   Utterly isolated from the rest of the world,
their only means of communication destroyed, their
condition was forlorn in the extreme.   In their outward circumstances they were tolerably comfortable,
as they had brought with them enough of the necessities of life to sustain them until the land could be
made to produce fresh supplies.   Such clothing as
they possessed would have to be carefully kept, and
as regarded the native men and women, the simplest
covering sufficed for them.   The land was shared out
among the Englishmen, their native servants helping
them to cultivate the ground.   Salt was obtained from
the small, shallow pools in the rocks, and these rocks
were also shared among them.

For two years a fair degree of prosperity blessed
their efforts, but the comparative peace and success
they enjoyed could not be expected to continue.   The
first real trouble and disturbance was caused by one
of the mutineers named Williams.   His wife had gone
out one day among the cliffs to search for sea birds

and eggs. While so doing, she fell and was killed. Williams, wanting another woman, demanded and obtained the wife of one of the native men. Wronged and outraged by this scandalous act, the native men vowed to be revenged on the Englishmen, and a plot was formed to murder them all. The secret being made known to the women, they imparted it to the Englishmen, in a song as follows:—

> "Why does black man sharpen ax?
> To kill white man."

And now begins a story of oppression, treachery, and bloodshed, that forms the darkest page in this island's history. So constant was the dread experienced by some of the women, that they contrived, in secret, to construct a rude raft, with the intention of returning to Tahiti, or be lost in the attempt. They had their raft launched, and ventured a little way beyond the breakers; but their hearts failed them, and the entreaties of some of the women left behind, who had found out their intention, prevailing, they returned to shore again. Hostile feelings were strong on both sides. The women, however, sided entirely with the Englishmen. In one instance one of the women deliberately murdered her native husband, when they were alone together in a cave where they lived.*

When some degree of peace had been restored, and the suspicions of their masters were quieted, the

---

*It is to this that Mr. Nobbs referred when, many years later, in his song entitled "Pitcairn," he speaks of the "ghost that still lingers on Tullaloo's Ridge." Tullaloo was the man's name.

wronged and oppressed Tahitians, obtaining possession of arms, fell upon the white men while they were
quietly working on their allotments of land, and
hunted and shot them down.   Fletcher Christian,
John Mills, Isaac Martin, William Brown, and John
Williams were killed.   William McCoy and Matthew
Quintall escaped into the woods, while John Adams,
having at first escaped into the woods, on again showing himself, was shot and severely wounded.   Recov-
ering himself, he ran away from his pursuers, and,
making for the rocky cliffs, would have thrown himself off, but those in pursuit, by sundry signs, showed
that they intended no further harm.   Being thus reassured of his safety, he returned with them to one of
the houses, where he was kindly treated.   Edward
Young, a favorite with the women, had been con-
cealed by them, and so escaped the dangers to which
the others had been exposed.   Thus were the lives of
four among the nine mutineers spared.   But peace was
not yet to be.   How was it possible, when the men and
women that remained practiced freely every vice that
could degrade manhood and womanhood.   Treachery
and bloodshed still raged among them, and no one felt
his life secure.

A story is told of how the death of one of the native
men was accomplished.   It was before anyone had
been killed.   The man, called by the name of Timiti, had been accused of some wrongdoing, and was
brought before the Englishmen to be tried.   Christian, so the story goes, was, while trying the case,

THE LANDING PLACE, BOUNTY BAY

walking backward and forward through the midst of the assembled company met to see the result of the trial. Timiti, learning only too well that his sentence would be death, took the opportunity when Christian was in the act of turning himself around, to make a spring for the open door. Before his judges could recover from their surprise, he was too far on his way to be readily overtaken, and his pursuers were obliged to return without him. Taking a short cut down towards the sea, he speedily descended the steep cliffs, and ran across the rocky shore. Swimming across places where no footpath could be found, and walking the rest of the way, he at length reached a place on the south side of the island known by the name of Taowtama. Here he succeeded in hiding himself for a while, until someone descried him from the heights above, engaged in a favorite pastime, called *ihara* (pronounced *e-hurra*).

The news soon spread that Timiti's hiding place was discovered, and another native, named Menálee, was sent out to secure him. One of his companions also went with him, and before long they were at the place. Timiti, suspecting treachery, would have fled, but the two men, through their fair speeches and the food they had brought him, quickly disarmed him of his suspicions. To further assure him they produced a comb, and prevailed on him to let them comb his hair. Having thus decoyed him into their power, the rest was easy enough, and a few seconds sufficed to dispatch the poor fellow.

After the massacre of Christian and his companions the native men turned upon one another, and the four remaining Englishmen, assisted by the widows of the murdered white men, joined in ridding the island of these "disturbers of the peace," so that in a short time after the mutineers had been killed every one of the native men was also put to death.

During the occurrence of these shocking scenes, how must every human impulse and every kindly feeling have been nearly extinguished! To add to the dreadful evils that were committed, McCoy, who had been brought up in a distillery, spent much of his time in distilling ardent spirits from the roots of the *tee* plant. Quintall assisted him, his "teakettle being converted into a still." These two men succeeded but too well. Drunkenness was added to the already long list of vices, and was of frequent occurrence. In McCoy's case it brought its own punishment, for in an attack of delirium he made his way to the rocky shore, and, fastening a stone around his body, cast himself off into the sea. The dead body was found by a little girl, a daughter of John Adams, and was brought up to the little settlement and buried.

Quintall, McCoy's boon companion, met his death at the hands of his two remaining shipmates. Always disorderly and troublesome, provoking a quarrel whenever he could, and frequently threatening the lives of Young and Adams, he became a constant terror to them. As an instance of his ferocious nature, the story is handed down that one day his wife went out fishing, and, not succeeding in obtaining enough to satisfy Quintall, he punished her by biting off her ear.*　Like Williams, he also lost his wife, and in the same way, she having fallen from the rocks when going after birds.　Regardless of the fearful conse-quences which so quickly followed a crime of the same nature only a short time before, Quintall de-manded the wife of one of his two remaining compan-ions.　Their refusal to comply with his demands determined him to try to put his oft-repeated threats into execution.　Adams and Young, knowing their lives to be in danger, felt themselves justified in put-ting an end to Quintall's life.

The opportunity soon came, and one day when he was in John Adams' house, he was set upon and overpowered by the two other men.　By means of a hatchet the dreadful work of death was soon com-pleted.　The daughter of John Mills (who lived to the age of ninety-three), then a young girl of eight or nine years of age, was an eyewitness of the awful deed, and used to relate how terrified were all of the little band of women and children who beheld the blood-bespattered walls.　The dreadful scene was vividly pictured on her mind and memory through the long course of more than eighty years.

*Asserted as a fact.

THE MUTINEERS DISCOVERED

CHAPTER III.

T HE two chief causes of trouble and mischief being now removed, there was prospect of enjoying more tranquillity and peace than had ever been known before. Of the fifteen males who landed on the island, only two now remained. These two, Adams and Young, having the whole responsibility of the young and increasing colony devolving upon them, arose to the exigency of the case. Young was naturally of a thoughtful and serious cast of mind, and the scenes which he and Adams had witnessed, and in which they had participated, had the effect of deepening the serious impressions that had been made upon them both, and they resolved to train, as best they could, their own children and those of their unfortunate companions, in the paths of virtue and right. Young's superior education better fitted him for the grave undertaking; but he did not long survive his repentance. He had long been afflicted with the asthma, and died of that complaint in the year 1800, about a year after Quintall's death.

John Adams was now sole survivor. With a deep and abiding repentance for his former course of life, he strove to amend the misdoings of years by instilling into the minds of the young and rising generation around him right principles. Alone and unaided in the gigantic task, he suffered not his courage to fail in the endeavor, and his earnestness of purpose, directed in a right channel, could not fail to win some measure of success. The number of children that had been born to the mutineers was twenty-three. Fletcher Christian left three children; John Mills, two: William McCoy, three; Matthew Quintall, five; Edward Young, six; and John Adams, four. John Williams, a Frenchman, Isaac Martin, an American, and William Brown, an Englishman, left no children.

John Adams used to relate that it was through the influence of a dream that he was first led seriously to consider the condition of the helpless and ignorant youths who were so suddenly and unexpectedly left on his hands, and to arouse himself to the heavy responsibility that rested on him, as the only instructor that could be had for them, totally unfit for the task though he might be. It was a late beginning, but he engaged in the work with all his heart. A Bible and prayer book saved from the *Bounty* were the only means at his command in teaching the young people to read. But, with the blessing of God upon his hum-

3

ble efforts, John Adams had the satisfaction of seeing the children of such disreputable parentage growing up around him, quiet, peaceable, industrious, and happy, and with an increasing love of virtue and strict morality. A beautiful feature of the whole was the love that united them as one family under the fatherly control of John Adams. Such was the condition of life on Pitcairn Island when, in 1808, Captain Mayhew Folger, of the American ship *Topaz*, accidentally discovered that the island was inhabited. Following is part of a letter received by the writer from Mr. Robert Folger (a son of the captain above named), who kindly gave permission to make use of it. The letter was dated Massillon, Stark County, Ohio, August 4, 1882. After giving his reasons for writing, the letter proceeds as follows:—

"My brother, sister, and myself are the only surviving children of Captain Mayhew Folger, of the ship *Topaz*, of Boston, the discoverer, in February, 1808, of the colony on Pitcairn's Island. I do not like to refer to the survivor of the *Bounty* crew on the island as a mutineer, for I cannot help feeling that the cruelty of Bligh to his men was such as to justify almost anything on the part of the people on board. . . . I may now say that I have been for nearly twenty-five years gathering facts in regard to Pitcairn's Island.

"I have Bligh's own account of the mutiny, 'Delano's Voyages,' my father's logbook, with his entry therein in his own handwriting, dated, as I now remember, February 8, 1808—Lady Belcher's book, 'The Mutineers of the *Bounty*'—and numerous letters and newspaper publications.

"If you would like a copy of my father's journal entry, I shall have great pleasure in transcribing it, and sending it to you. I may as well say in advance that he, as a shipmaster, shared in the general feeling of the world, and shipmasters especially, against the 'arch-mutineer,' Christian.

"The history of your island will long, I may say always, be a wonder. During the sixty years that I remember it, it has been a wonder, and it will continue to be, as wonders do not decrease in interest. Three-quarters of a century have gone into the great ocean of time since Captain Mayhew Folger discovered the colony, and the interest in the history of the island is unabated. The island cannot be mentioned without exciting a wonder even in the mind of the unlearned, as to the history of the colonists, their present status, and, indeed, all that concerns them.

"In connection with the truth concerning the colonists, there has been a great deal of error and nonsense published. *Blackwood's Magazine* is not free from being a participant in setting afloat most senseless statements, which were about twenty-four years since repeated in this country. There are very few living who can enter into the *spirit* of Pitcairn's history, and, what is to me most singular and unaccountable, a large number of would-be historians are engaged in uttering most senseless pretensions to correct the history of the island, from the arrival of the *Bounty* until the arrival of the *Topaz*—a period of twenty years when nothing was known, nor could be known, of the island, nor was known until the arrival of the *Topaz* in February, 1808.

"You, undoubtedly, have had access to the account of the mutiny by Captain Bligh, also to 'Delano's Voyages,' published in 1817, in which are two letters from Captain Folger, one to Captain Delano, and one to the Lords of the Admiralty, R. N., and which was received by them through Rear Admiral Hotham, who, in 1813, was, I think, in command of the English blockading squadron on our coast in the War of 1812. . . . It was through Rear Admiral Hotham that my father sent the Azimuth compass, and within five years last past I have noticed in some publication (I cannot state what one) that Her Majesty's navy had obtained the *Bounty's* chronometer, which was taken from my father at Valparaiso when his vessel was confiscated by the Spanish governor of Chile when he reached the South American Coast, after having visited Pitcairn's Island.

"As your grandfather, Mr. Buffett, mentions 'Delano's Voyages,' I suppose you too have read that, in many respects, curious book. In the main, the portion which refers to my father is correct. Captain Delano visited my father at Kendal in 1817. . . . In reading Mr. Delano's book you will find a letter to the Lords of the Admiralty dated at Kendal. . . . If I were to write a history of the island, I could give a chronological statement that would be in order and critically correct, as I think I have in my library every date from the discovery of the island in 1767, by Captain Cartaret, of H. B. M. ship *Swallow*, to the present time. . . .

"Since writing the foregoing, I concluded to copy all the entries from my father's logbook in which the island is mentioned. . . .

"'Ship *Topaz*, of Boston, Mayhew Folger master, on a sealing voyage to the South Pacific Ocean, 1808.

"'Saturday, 6th February.—First part light airs at east, steering west by south, half south by compass. At ½ past on P. M. saw land bearing southwest by west half west. Steered for the land with a light breeze at east, the said land being Pitcairn's Island, discovered

BOUNTY BAY FROM THE CLIFFS.

in 1767 by Captain Cartaret in his Britannic Majesty's
sloop *Swallow*. A 2 A. M. the isle bore south two
leagues distant. Lay off and on till daylight. At 6
A. M. put off with two boats to explore and look for
seals.

"'On approaching the shore saw a smoke on the
land, at which I was very much surprised, it being
represented by Captain Cartaret as destitute of inhabitants.

"'On approaching still nearer the land, I discovered
a boat paddling towards me with three men in her.
On approaching her, they hailed me in the English
language, asking who was the captain of the ship, and
offered me a number of cocoanuts, which they had
brought off as a present, and requested I would land,
there being, as they said, a white man on shore.

"' I went on shore and found there an Englishman
by the name of Alexander Smith, the only person
remaining out of nine that escaped on board the ship
Bounty, Captain Bligh, under the command of that
arch-mutineer, Christian. Smith informed me that,
after putting Captain Bligh in the longboat and sending her adrift, Commander Christian proceeded to
Otaheite. There all the mutineers chose to stop
except Christian himself, Smith, and seven others.
They all took wives at Otaheite, and six men as servants, and proceeded to Pitcairn's Island, where they
landed all their goods and chattels, ran the ship *Bounty*
on shore, and broke her up, which took place, as near
as he could recollect, in 1790. Soon after, one of their
party ran mad and drowned himself; another died with
a fever, and after they had remained about four years
on the island, their men servants rose upon them and
killed six of them, leaving only Smith alive, and he
desperately wounded, with a pistol ball in the neck.
However, he and the widows of the deceased arose

and put all the servants to death, which left him the only surviving man on the island, with eight or nine women and several small children. He immediately went to work tilling the ground, so that it produces plenty for them all, and he lives very comfortably as commander-in-chief of Pitcairn's Island.*

"'All the children of the deceased mutineers speak tolerable English; some of them are grown to the size of men and women; and, to do them justice, I think them a very humane and hospitable people; and whatever may have been the errors or crimes of Smith, the mutineer, in times back, he is at present a worthy man, and may be useful to navigators who traverse this immense ocean.

"'Such is the history of Christian and his associates. Be it remembered that this island is scantily supplied with fresh water, so that it is impossible for a ship to get a supply. I place it in latitude 25° 2' south, and 130° west longitude, from my last lunar observation.

"'Sunday, 7 February.—Light airs from the eastward and very hot. The ship laying off and on, I stayed on shore with the friendly Smith and his truly good people until 4 P. M., then left them and went on board and made sail, steering southeast and southeast by east, bound for Massafuero, having received from the people on shore some hogs, cocoanuts, and plantains. At noon the isle bore northwest by north by compass 34' dist. Latitude observation 25° 31' south, etc.'"

After Captain Folger's accidental discovery of the little colony on Pitcairn Island, nothing more was

---

*There is a little difference between Captain Folger's statement and the real facts of those early days, as handed down through succeeding generations, from those (especially Susanna, the girl of fifteen from Tahiti) who were eye-witnesses of the dreadful scenes that took place, when bloodshed followed treachery in their dealings between master and servant.

known or heard of them for a period of nearly six years. In the year 1814 H. M. ships *Briton* and *Tagus*, commanded respectively by Captains Staines and Pipon, out on a cruise and returning to Valparaiso from the Marquesas, passed near the island. So strange was the sight of a ship that when these two were first descried approaching the island, the young woman who first saw them ran to make it known to the rest by saying that "two *paafata* [a wooden flooring erected on four posts, on which the feed for their goats was kept] were floating in toward the shore, with their posts turned wrong end up." But the experienced eye of John Adams soon discerned what the visitors were.

As for the people on board, they were not a little surprised to see from their vessels the land laid out in regular plantations. The houses, too, that could be seen were different in make from those of the other islands they had lately visited. In a short time a canoe was seen paddling off towards the ships. To the astonishment of those on board, the visitors from the shore, on coming near enough to speak to those on the *Briton*, called out in plain English, "Won't you heave us a rope now?" A rope was thrown them, and they were warmly welcomed on board.

The mystery was explained when, on being questioned, they said that they were Thursday October Christian, son of Fletcher Christian, the mutineer, and George Young, son of the midshipman Edward Young. The former was named after the day and

month of his birth.   He was described as a "tall and
handsome young man about twenty-four years of age,
his scanty clothing consisting of a waistcloth, while he
wore a broad-brimmed straw hat adorned with black
cock's feathers."   His companion, George Young, was
said to be a "fine, noble-looking youth, 17 or 18 years
of age."   On being invited below, and having food set
before them, they further astonished their kind entertainers by reverently asking a blessing before par-
taking of their food.   In reply to a question they said
that the good custom had been taught them by John
Adams.   Every kindness was shown to the two young
men, and when they were taken to see a cow that was
on board the ship, they created some amusement by
asking whether the animal was "a huge goat or a
horned sow."

Captain Sir Thomas Staines went on shore, and was
agreeably surprised to find the youthful colony living
harmoniously together under the patriarchal rule of
John Adams.   Great fears were entertained by the
humble islanders lest their only instructor and teacher
should be removed from them, more especially as he
had fully decided to give himself up should he be
required to do so.   But the Tahitian women pleaded
strongly that he might be allowed to remain, and,
clinging to John Adams, weeping while they pleaded,
the humane captain, himself deeply touched at the
scene, resolved not to disturb them.   At the same
time he advised Adams not to go down to the landing
place, where the boat was, himself making the excuse

THURSDAY OCTOBER CHRISTIAN.

that the path to the beach was sufficiently rough and
stony for the old man not to venture. The advice was
followed, Adams accompanying the kind-hearted captain only part of the way. Thanking him for the
thoughtful consideration shown to himself and people,
he bade Captain Staines farewell, and returned to the
little village.

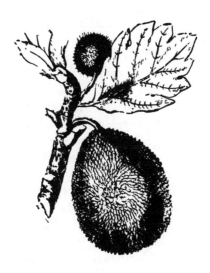

THE GEM of the PACIFIC

CHAPTER IV.

ITCAIRN ISLAND, brought to notice through the events already narrated, is insignificantly small, being only about five miles and a half in circumference and two miles and a half across. It was, when the mutineers first settled on it, thickly covered with trees wherever there was soil sufficient for their roots to take hold; but, in the period of a hundred years, during which wild goats have roamed in herds over certain portions of the island, many of the trees have disappeared. The soil, thus made bare, has severely suffered by being washed away by heavy rains, and scarcely a trace of the once luxuriant growth of trees remains. Viewed from the sea, the island in twŏ or three places presents a bare and sterile appearance. Its isolated position in mid-ocean, its rock-bound shores and precipitous cliffs, alike impress the beholder with a sense of the security such a place would afford to those whose chief aim was to hide their crimes and get beyond the reach of well-merited punishment.

The highest part of the island is about one thousand one hundred and nine feet above the sea. Facing the north is a peak, or immense rock, scarcely less high, called the Goat House. A cave in the side of this rock, partly hidden by lofty trees, is said to have been the intended retreat of Christian and his companions, in the event of their being sought after and their lone island discovered. The peak overlooking Bounty Bay, called Ship-landing Point, because it stands directly over the place where the *Bounty* was driven near the rocks and destroyed, has been described as "possessing considerable beauty." It rises in bold outline almost perpendicularly from the sea, its rugged, rocky front softened here and there by patches of grass and shrubs. The scenery surrounding the little bay, with its rocky shore, is always beautiful. Vine-covered trees, with foliage of intensest green—more especially the *pandanus* palm tree—flourish in rich growth quite near the water's edge, the salt spray frequently moistening their branches, while the soft sea air helps to diffuse the delicious fragrance of the sweetest flower that the island boasts of, the *morinda citrifolia*, named by the islanders simply "high white," in distinction to the pure white blossoms of the "four o'clock," which blooms on a low bush.

Overhead, near the highest extremity of Ship-landing Point, looking from the north, is seen a natural

curiosity, a huge portion of the rock showing in pro-
file a representation of a man's head of gigantic size.
It is called the Old Man's Head, and it is not difficult
to imagine that it looks down upon the small bay
with an expression of mild benevolence. The ascent
from the landing place is very steep, but is made com-
paratively easy by a very tolerable road leading up
the few hundred feet.

On the southeast side of the island is the place
known as "the Rope," so called because in former
years the steep descent could only be accomplished
by means of a rope. A zigzag path, only wide enough
to afford a foothold, now leads down from the high
precipice to the water's edge. The steep cliffs, rising
almost perpendicularly from the shore, are grandly
beautiful. The variegated colors of the soil, the rocks,
and the foliage of trees, all blended together, or con-
trasted in shades of black and gray, yellow and brown,
red and green, make the scenery altogether pleasing;
and not less beautiful is the view of the waters of the
little bay, when, calm and smooth, it spreads out like
a lake, without a ripple on its surface, or when, with
wild and roaring sound, wave after wave breaks and
rolls in toward the shore, leaving the surface of the
water as if covered with billows of loveliest lace, pure
and white.

In the most sheltered corner of the bay, at the Rope,
is a small stretch of sand, on one end of which, at the
foot of the rock that towers above it, there were found
by the mutineers some stone axes and other imple-

PATH THROUGH COCOANUT GROVE.

ments, which were made and used by the natives that originally inhabited the island.   Here, too, are cut in the rocks some of the figures made by the rude artists of those b y - g o n e ages.   Most of the characters h a v e been obliterated by more than a century's exposure to e v e r y k i n d of weather.   A few, however,   remain quite distinct, as may be seen by the accompanying illustration.

FIGURES CUT IN THE ROCKS AT THE ROPE.

The *pandanus* palm tree, with its clustering branches of drooping leaves, fringes the shores of the bay nearly its whole extent.   The innumerable huge stones and rocks that cover the bottom of the bay make it impossible for a boat to land.   Its waters teem with myriads of small fish.   The bèche de mer drags out its existence in the many sand-bottomed pools, while the cray fish and whelk, both of which are eaten, make their home beneath and among the seaweed-covered ròcks that abound in the shallow bay.   Looking north from the ridge of the Rope, the eye rests upon a small but lovely valley, named St.

Paul's Valley, it being in the vicinity of St. Paul's Rock. Grand old trees, with their varied and changing tints of foliage, render the scenery always beautiful, while, as an accompaniment to their gentle, rustling music, comes the booming sound of the surf on the rocks far below.

In the valley between Ship-landing Point on the northeast and the Goat House, facing north, lies, nestling among trees, the little village settled by the mutineers a hundred years ago. Groves of cocoanut and orange trees surround it, while the beautiful banyan tree, with its curious growth of long, rope-like roots hanging in thick profusion, and its towering branches covered for ten months of the year with a springlike robe of green, lends a delightful charm to the scenery.

Although the island is rocky to some extent, it still possesses much picturesque beauty. Steep ridges and deep valleys are its chief characteristics, both being covered by grand old shade-giving trees. The only drawback to a thorough enjoyment of walking or resting beneath the trees is the absence of singing birds to enliven the branches with their songs. One little homely bird with its coat of brown and white is the only occupant of the woods, with the exception of a beautiful white sea bird that in the early warmer season comes to deposit its egg on a niche of the bare branch of the banyan or other large tree. These two birds, the former with its constant "tweet, tweet," and the latter with its lively, shrill calls, impart some life to the otherwise silent groves. Occasionally a few other varieties of sea birds, sailing overhead, pierce the silent air with their cries.

Ferns, of which there are about twenty-six varieties, adorn the valleys in lovely and rich profusion. Of wild flowers there are but few, and all of them are, with one exception, small, white, and fragrant. This one is a sweet little flower that loves to open its golden eyes during the colder months of the year, and is found mostly around the edge of the high precipices.

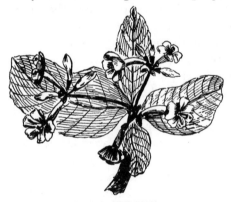

MORINDA CITRIFOLIA.

It is a universal favorite. The "flower tree" (*morinda citrifolia*) is in bloom almost all the year round, but is at its loveliest from October to March. Its pure white blossoms contrast richly with the dark, glossy leaves, while its delightful perfume, as well as its simple beauty, makes it a favorite with old and young. Children, boys as well as girls, find a never-ceasing pleasure in stringing the flowers into garlands, which they wear around their hats.

The bright blossoms that here and there meet the
eye have been introduced from time to time, mostly
by the captains of passing ships, who have kindly
given from their own limited stock.   Also many
seeds have been sent by friends in England, America,
and the Sandwich Islands; but only those from the
last-named place have succeeded well, most of the
others, owing greatly, no doubt, to the want of proper
culture, having proved a failure.   However, through
the thoughtful kindness of friends, the little island is
not entirely destitute of nature's loveliest productions.

First among the principal fruits that the island produces is the orange.   The trees begin to be in blossom from the end of July at the earliest, and continue
flowering until October.   The season of the fruit is
from April to November.   As the trees occasionally
produce a second crop, it is not unusual to have them
in fruit the year round.   Watermelons, muskmelons,
pineapples, roseapples, and figs are in season from
November to April.   Bananas, of which there are a
few varieties, can be had all the year round, but are at
their best from January to June.   The guava grows
wild, and from March to July the trees are laden with
fruit.   Grapes might be cultivated.   The sugar cane
is also one of the principal productions of the island,
the rich syrup made from its juice being used instead
of sugar.   Arrowroot is cultivated with profit.   The
process of making it involves much labor.   The
plants are set in the ground in the months of October
and November, and the roots are fully matured by

June. The yam crop is set at the same time as the arrowroot, and takes the same length of time to come to maturity.

Such are some of the present productions of the little island that became the hiding place of the mutineers. They themselves doubtless introduced the breadfruit, cocoanut, taro, yam, and one variety of the sweet potato. The places they once owned and cultivated are still called by their names, as John Adams' Breadfruit Patch, Ned Young's Ground, McCoy's Valley, and so on through the whole list. But, while their names remain, every trace of their burial places is lost, the grave of John Adams alone excepted.

Pitcairn! To thee, land of my birth,
  My song I bring;
Thy hills and valleys, trees and flowers,
  Their praise I sing.

The cocoanut, with waving plumes
  Of shining green,
The sweetly-scented orange blooms,
  Both here are seen.

And stately trees, and luscious fruits,
  Thy soil supplies;
But the enriching showers and rains
  The heaven denies.

Thou once wast fertile, rich, and green,
  But now, how bare;
And yet thou still art beautiful,
  Still sweet and fair.

Such matchless days of calm, fair skies
  Thy summers bring!
And lovely, too, are all the hours
  Of balmy spring.

Each season, as it rolls around,
  New beauties gives;
And every object, silent, cries,
  "My Maker lives."

JOHN BUFFETT and JOHN EVANS

MARRIAGES and BIRTHS

CHAPTER V.

O return to John Adams and his small community. Five or six years had passed since the visits of the *Briton* and the *Tagus*, and during that time the fact of the island being inhabited, and by whom, had become more widely known. About the year 1819 the East India Company's ship *Hercules*, Captain Henderson, made a call at the island and left some useful and much-needed gifts for the islanders, consisting of carpenters' tools, large iron boilers, etc., etc., the last mentioned being used chiefly for the purpose of boiling down salt water to obtain salt.

In the month of October, 1823, an English whale-ship, the *Cyrus*, Captain Hall, visited Pitcairn Island. John Adams, being now somewhat advanced in years, and beginning already to feel the infirmities of age, expressed to Captain Hall the wish that he could find among the ship's crew someone to assist him in the arduous task of trying to impart instruction to his young people. The captain listened kindly, and promised to do what he could. Calling his men around him, he made known to them the wishes of the old man, and asked if any of them would be willing to accede to his request. After a few minutes' hesitation, John Buffett, a young man twenty-six years of age, stepped forward and volunteered his services. Being bound by no home ties, he counted it no great sacrifice to remain.

Buffett had in early youth been apprenticed to a cabinet maker in Bristol, his native place. Of a roving disposition, a sea life especially possessing a peculiar fascination for him, he left his early trade to serve on board His Majesty's ship *Penelope*, and again on the *Impregnable*. He was shipwrecked in the Gulf of St. Lawrence, and afterwards cast away on the coast of California, where he was received and cared for in the kindest manner by an old Spanish *comandante* in the place. The latter made every effort to persuade Buffett to make his home in California, but he decided not to do so, and from thence he made his way to Honolulu, in the Sandwich Islands, where he joined the *Cyrus*. At last, after his many adventures, he arrived at Pitcairn Island, where, accepting his captain's proposal, he resolved to end his days among the people with whom his lot was now cast.

Among his shipmates on board the *Cyrus* was a youth about nineteen years of age, named John Evans, a native of London. For love of Buffett, he determined to remain on the island, and for this purpose he

ran away from the ship.   Being of very small build,
he contrived to hide himself in the hollow stump of a
tree until the vessel had sailed, and it was safe for him
to make his appearance.   As there was no help for it,
Evans also was allowed to become a member of the
community.

Not many months passed before both Buffett and
Evans sought in marriage the hands of two of the
island maidens.   Buffett met with no opposition to his
suit, and, in due time, was united in marriage to Dor-
othy, a daughter of Edward Young.   Evans did not
obtain such ready favor when he requested of John
Adams the hand of his daughter Rachel.   The old
man did not approve of the young people's entering
the marriage relation at too early an age, and Evans
was barely nineteen; besides, the disparity in age of
the two young persons was another obstacle in the
father's view, the young woman being the older by
some years.   However, the matter was referred to the
daughter for decision.   Her answer came, quick, short,
and decided, "Try it, daddy."   He at length consented,
but not without misgivings regarding her future happiness, and his paternal blessing was not withheld when
the twain stood up to be made one, being wedded with
a ring formed of the outer circle of a limpet shell.

It may prove interesting to some readers to know
the names of those others whom John Adams united
in the bonds of matrimony.   The service was performed according to the rites of the Church of England.   The parties were, of course, the sons and

THE CHAPEL

daughters of all the mutineers who left children, and
their names are as follows: Matthew Quintall to
Elizabeth Mills, Arthur Quintall to Katharine McCoy,
Daniel McCoy to Sarah Quintall. These two last mentioned young men one day swam off to a rock at a considerable distance from the shore, and there agreed to
seek each one the other's sister for a wife. The rock
received, from that incident, its name, *Táné M'á, i. e.*,
"The place of the men's agreement." Thursday October Christian, son of Fletcher Christian, and the first
born on the island, married Susan, the girl of fifteen
who came in the *Bounty*. The others were: Charles
Christian, married to Sarah McCoy; Edward Quintall,
to Dinah Adams; George Young, to Hannah Adams;
William Young, to Elizabeth Mills, widow of Matthew
Quintall, who met his death in some unknown manner.
Most of the young men went out one day in their
canoes to fish. They were mostly within speaking
distance of each other, but as Matthew, or Matt, as he
was called, was not seen tending his canoe, the others
supposed that he was lying down in it. It was afterwards discovered that the canoe was, and had been no
one knew how long, floating about without an occupant. The body had sunk, and was never again seen.

The following story is told to show the binding force
with which a promise was regarded in those early days:
George Adams, the only son of John Adams, had,
when quite a youth, "conceived an attachment for Polly
Young, but she declared that she would never marry
George." On Captain Beechy's visit to the island,

Adams referred the case to him and the other officers. Their opinion was that the young girl's determination was made before she was old enough to know her own mind, and would be more "honored in the breach than the observance." Polly, however, viewed the matter in a different light, but confessed that her opinion of her lover was considerably altered since she declared she would not have him. Subsequently they were married, perhaps not "in haste," but Polly repented "in a hurry," for she discovered all too soon that a home with George did not mean a "woman's paradise."

One gold ring, the property of Edward Young, played an important part in the wedding services performed in those days, and continued to be used until somewhere in the forties.

Only four of the children of the mutineers died unmarried. One of them, Johnny, the only son of John Mills, the mutineer, came to his death by an awful fall from a high, rocky cliff, where he had gone in search of birds' eggs. His injuries were such that he died before he could be conveyed to his home. The poor lad was only fourteen years old when the sad accident occurred. Two of the sons of Edward Young, Robert and Edward, both died shortly after the return of the community from Tahiti in 1831, while Fletcher Christian's only daughter, Mary, died of dropsy, on Norfolk Island, about the year 1865. A daughter of Quintall, having strayed from the path of virtue, was so harshly treated by her brother that when she had an opportunity she left the island. The captain of a passing vessel, being informed of the matter, and learning the wish of the unfortunate young woman, kindly allowed her a passage on his ship. She was taken to the island of Rurutu, where she was most kindly received. One of the chiefs of the island made her his wife, and she eventually became the mother of a numerous family.

Such were the early loves and marriages between the children of the original settlers. Families of healthy, vigorous children were raised, and over them all John Adams presided, much after the fashion of the patriarchs of old, and was looked up to and respected as a father by the growing community, who had the utmost confidence in the wisdom of his counsels and teachings. At the time of Captain Beechy's visit in the *Blossom*, in 1825, the community numbered twenty-six adults and thirty-five children, making a total of sixty-one persons. During a period of thirty-five years there had been twenty-seven births, and of the original settlers from the *Bounty* there remained only John Adams and five of the Tahitian women. These six, with the addition of Buffett and Evans, made eight of the adult population.

When it was first ascertained that the *Blossom* was a man-of-war, great fears prevailed among the little community lest the ship had come to convey Adams a prisoner to England. But they were soon reassured. The captain and officers hastened to explain that their coming was for an altogether different purpose. When they realized that their fears were groundless,

and that there was no danger of the old man's removal,
the female portion of the community crowded around
him and embraced him in the most affectionate manner.   Especially touching it was to see the way in
which Hannah Young clung to her father and embraced him, weeping, even, in the fullness of her joy
when she understood that he was not to be taken
away.

GROUP OF ISLAND MAIDENS.

During the whole stay of the *Blossom* her captain
and officers were most hospitably entertained by the
simple-hearted islanders. The young women especially, who inherited from their Tahitian mothers a

strong love for flowers, made it their pleasant duty every morning to adorn the caps of the officers with freshly-made wreaths of sweet-smelling flowers. The visitors were charmed with the open, simple manners of all the islanders, but observed that "the same marked difference between the sexes prevailed here as in all the islands of the Pacific, notably at meals, the women were not allowed to sit down with the men; and when the captain and officers passed their remarks and opinions respecting the difference observed between the sexes, their words were resented, as seeming to interfere with long-established custom." (It was not so much a "marked difference between the sexes" as a feeling of unaccountable shyness that prevented the women in those early times from sitting down to the same table with strangers. At the present day most of the island women, inheriting the same dispositions from their mothers, when an occasional visitor happens to share their hospitality, would much prefer to "stand and wait" than act the part of hostess by sitting down with their guests.)

The day was invariably begun and ended with prayer and praise to the divine Father for His mercies and His preserving care, each and every family engaging in a short service of worship by parents and children, nor was a day considered as rightly begun if their first duty to their Creator was omitted. This right custom has ever been, and still is, religiously observed by their descendants. Captain Beechy and his officers had the opportunity during their stay of attending

5

divine service on the Sunday. That day was very strictly kept. There was complete cessation from work; no fires were made, all the cooking being done on the Saturday, that nothing of a worldly nature might interfere with the sacred duties of the day of rest. In the public worship on Sundays, Buffett assisted Adams in reading the service, the especial part allotted him being the sermon, "some sentences of which were read over two or three times," to catch the attention of his hearers, and also to help to impress the words on their memory. Buffett also acted as schoolmaster, and "found the children both willing and attentive scholars."

When the *Blossom* left the island, the tearful, affectionate farewells told how the hearts of all the islanders had been won to their visitors, whose pleasant stay and cheerful companionship had been such a bright spot in their quiet lives, and was to form ever after one of their most delightful and pleasing recollections.

GEORGE HUN NOBBS

DEATH OF JOHN ADAMS

CHAPTER VI.

HE even, uneventful round of life in the little community passed steadily along, with "scarcely a ripple to stir its monotonous surface." Cultivating the ground and keeping it in order, building houses for the more newly married couples, canoe building and fishing, and occasionally going out with their guns to shoot goats, wild fowl, and birds, supplied constant occupation for the men. A favorite mode of taking fish was with the spear, usually made by fastening five pieces of iron, bent to the required shape, and having barbed points, onto a pole about twenty feet long, and in the use of which the men were very expert. The women were always to be seen assisting their husbands, fathers, and brothers in their outdoor occupations, and sometimes accompanied them when they went out in their canoes to fish. Cooking and other housework, and taking care of the children, gave them daily employment. But their principal work, during the colder months of the year, was the making of native cloth.

This native cloth, or *tappa*, is made from the bark of the *aute* plant (pronounced outy), *i. e.*, the paper mulberry, and has very much the nature and consistency of paper. The work is exceedingly laborious and wearisome, and when the yield of the plants is large, it sometimes occupies months in doing. Yet it was necessary to be done, as that material supplied nearly all the bedding used then.

When anyone not accustomed to sleeping beneath such noise-creating bedclothes tries it for the first time, the constant loud rustle that it makes generally succeeds in driving all sleep away. Captain Beechy spoke of sleeping in cloth that "seemed fresh from the loom," as that was all that his entertainers could give him. Frequent washing and exposure to the sun will eventually deprive the material of its stiffness and noisiness, and in cold weather it affords a warm covering, as it excludes all air. It is colored a bright reddish brown, and rendered tougher by being dyed in the sap obtained from the *doodooee* (candlenut tree). This dye is made by steeping the bark of the *doodooee* in water.

In the early days this stiff, uncomfortable cloth was worn by all, with, perhaps, the exception of John Adams himself. By the women, pieces about a yard in width and two yards in length were fastened around the waist by simply crossing the two upper ends and turning them in to secure them. Another yard of the same material was thrown across the shoulders, as a covering to the body, and this constituted almost wholly their everyday garment. For Sunday wear each woman and girl owned a frock of most primitive make, being gathered in around the neck, and falling loosely from the shoulders, reaching a little below the knee. Underneath was a petticoat worn as described above, which completed the whole attire. The men and boys wore the waistcloth, almost exclusively, on week days. Sundays they donned their breeches, which did not reach to the knee, thus displaying the muscular growth of their limbs.

The frequent outdoor employments of both men and women resulted in a great muscular development of their physical frame, and rendered them strong and capable of enduring a vast amount of manual labor. Yet this did not deprive the female portion of the community of their feminine instincts, and all their womanly ways remained. Their children were brought up early to help in all the little homely duties that pertained to the house, as well as to aid their parents in field work; nor were they allowed to absent themselves from the school, where they were taught reading, writing, and arithmetic by John Buffett.

In 1828 George Hun Nobbs, accompanied by an American named Bunker, arrived at Pitcairn Island from Valparaiso. He had reached the last-mentioned place after having passed through several adventures, and while there heard for the first time the story of the *Bounty*, and how Pitcairn Island was settled by

the descendants of the mutineers.   The story so fas-
cinated him that he determined, if it could be done, to
reach the island and take up his residence with the
inhabitants.   Accordingly, obtaining possession of a
launch, he, with Bunker, left Valparaiso, and in due
time they reached their destination safely.   Both these
additions to their number received a cordial welcome
from the inhabitants.

Nobbs did not long delay seeking to woo and win
a wife; and, with some difficulty, at length succeeded
in obtaining the hand of Sarah Christian, a granddaughter of Fletcher Christian.   Bunker was not so
fortunate, for Peggy Christian would not listen to his
suit, and whether through unrequited love or a fit of
temporary insanity is not known, but he attempted
self-destruction by throwing himself headlong off a
cliff.   By some means the fall was broken, and his
suicidal intentions were frustrated.   He died, however,
shortly after.

The launch on which the voyage of the two men
was made was run ashore, broken up, and used in
building Nobbs' house.   In giving an account of himself, Nobbs said that he was the "unacknowledged son
of a marquis."   Being, by a superior education, better
fitted than was John Buffett to fill the place of teacher
among the youth of the island, Nobbs had not been
long among them before he took charge of the school,
taking the work almost entirely out of Buffett's hands.
Buffett was inclined to resent this act of Nobbs as a
gross injustice, but the people in general favored the

ROSA YOUNG.   ARTHUR YOUNG.
JOHN YOUNG.   SARAH YOUNG.

change, chiefly because of a grave fault which Buffett
had committed. Yet some of the parents remained
faithful in their allegiance to the teacher that had first
come among them, and did not withdraw their children from his care, for, in spite of his fault, he endeav-
ored to the best of his ability to perform his duty
faithfully to them, while he sought to atone for the
wrong he had done by a lifelong repentance.

The duty of officiating as pastor was also assumed
by Nobbs. John Adams had by this time left the
management of everything that concerned the progress and improvement of the people, in the hands of
the two younger men. On the twenty-ninth day of
March, 1829, the year following the arrival of Nobbs,
the last of the Englishmen that came in the *Bounty*
passed quietly and peacefully away, at the age of
sixty-five years, deeply and sincerely mourned by the
family over whom he had been so strangely placed.
He survived the last of his companions twenty-nine
years. A plain white stone marks his resting place,
the inscription "In Hope" being placed beneath the
simple record of his name, age, and death. The headstone was made in Devonport, England.

A year subsequent to the death of John Adams the
Seringapatam, man-of-war, Captain Waldegrave, visited the island, bringing gifts of clothing and other
useful presents to the islanders. Previous to that time
the people, on account of their rapidly increasing
numbers, had been considering whether the island,
with its limited resources, would be adequate to their

support and maintenance, not the least cause of anxiety being the scarcity of water. This condition of affairs was reported to the proper authorities, and an arrangement having been effected between the British Government and the authorities at Tahiti for a grant of land for the use of the Pitcairners in Tahiti, the *Comet*, sloop, Captain Sandilands, arrived at Pitcairn Island on the twenty-eighth day of February, 1831, as convoy to the *Lucy Ann*, which, on the seventh day of March, sailed for Tahiti, with the whole Pitcairn Island colony, and their small stock of movable goods, on board.

At the end of fourteen days the emigrants landed, having received a cordial welcome. But the experiment did not succeed. They had not been long in Tahiti when a malignant fever broke out amongst them and rapidly reduced their numbers. Fourteen of the people died in quick succession, and, notwithstanding the liberal provision made for their support by the kind-hearted people of Tahiti, the Pitcairners were anxiously desirous to return to their home. Then, too, the manners of the people among whom they now lived were so different from the pure, simple lives they led amongst themselves, and the open and undisguised immorality of some of the people around them rendered them very unhappy. In less than three weeks after their arrival at Tahiti an opportunity of returning presented itself, and Buffett and his family availed themselves of it. Four more of the young men accompanied them. The vessel that carried them called at Hood's Island on the way, and there one of the four young men died. After the safe arrival home of the others, and before the rest of the community came, another of their number passed away.

Meanwhile, preparations were making at Tahiti for the return of the rest of the people. The schooner *Charles Doggett* was chartered to convey them to their home. A quantity of the *Bounty's* copper had been carried to Tahiti, and this was given by the people to purchase the schooner, as it was all they were able to do; but liberal aid was given by generous friends in Tahiti, who raised a subscription to supply the deficiency. The return voyage occupied twenty-two days, the whole stay at Tahiti not extending over five months.

A pleasing incident is here recorded, illustrating the old Bible truth, "Cast thy bread upon the waters; for thou shalt find it after many days." During the sojourn of the Pitcairners at Tahiti, in the time of their deep sorrow and grief, when one and another of their number sickened and died, the second mate of an American whaleship, whose name was Coffin, learned of the dire distress that they suffered. Pitying their forlorn condition as strangers in a strange land, and obeying the impulse of a kind heart, he generously spent five dollars in procuring such food for those who were sick as he thought they would relish. Nor were the needs of the others forgotten. This act of disinterested Christian kindness was warmly remembered by all the people, and when, after nineteen years, the kind-hearted man came to Pitcairn as master of a ship, the people made him a present of ten barrels of yams, the cost of which was twenty dollars. This substantial proof of the recollection of his goodness toward them affected the captain to tears, and it was with difficulty that he could be prevailed upon to accept the gift, pleading that his former kindness might be allowed to pass unrewarded. But the people earnestly insisted upon his accepting what they considered but a small return for the unforgotten deed of kindness shown them in their extremity.

MR. JOSHUA HILL

CHAPTER VII.

A NEW chapter now opens in the history of this island. About the year 1832-33 it was favored with a new arrival, in the person of Joshua Hill. He was a man of excellent education, but stern in his nature, and a tyrannically strict disciplinarian. He reached the island by way of Tahiti, to which place he had come from Honolulu. In England he had heard the curious story of the little island in mid ocean, and how it was peopled, and he left home for the purpose of coming amongst the islanders as their pastor and teacher, considering his age no obstacle, although he was about seventy years old. But he was forestalled by Nobbs.

It is only fair to acknowledge that at the time of his coming the condition of affairs on the island did not witness favorably to the management of those who

(75)

were the acknowledged leaders. Like the Israelites in the times of the judges, "every man did what was right in his own eyes," for, since the patriarchal rule of John Adams, no one had supplied, as he did, the place he held so long in the confidence, as well as the affection, of the people.

It excites a feeling of surprise that, in all the old man's endeavors at reformation, he had allowed the old still, used by McCoy and Quintall, to continue its unholy, debasing work. But so it was; and at the time of Hill's arrival, it was in constant operation, several of the men being addicted to the vice; nor were Nobbs and Buffett averse to "a wee drap on the sly." Neither, since the removal to Tahiti, did all the people retain the beautiful, strict morality that had been their crowning virtue, as was proved in two cases; so that, altogether, the island stood in need of a general and thorough reformation.

Hill at once assumed the reins of government. His first step was to appoint four principal men to support him, to whom he gave the title of elders. These were supplemented by three sub-elders, and four cadets. The people at first willingly submitted to all his innovations, and, had he been as wise and prudent in the administration of his measures as he was zealous in having them performed, there is no question but that he would have accomplished such lasting good among the people as would have continued so long as they had a history. One fact will show that this was done, in spite of the many faults and errors that he committed during his brief term of leadership. To his honor be it recorded that through his untiring and energetic exertions the trouble-creating still was destroyed, and never after was its baleful work to be revived.

Hill professed to have been sent out by the English Government, which assertion, if not entirely false, was at least doubtful. He utterly ignored the presence of the other Englishmen, and succeeded only too well in influencing the islanders against them. But there was one exception. Charles Christian, a son of Fletcher Christian, whose many noble qualities endeared him to all, ever remained the staunch, unchanging friend of the persecuted Nobbs, Buffett, and Evans; and when, by Hill's order, Buffett was publicly flogged, this true friend, hearing of the unjust and cruel treatment, hastened to the rescue, and, by his unflinching bravery and manly courage, succeeded in delivering the unhappy man from his hard-hearted and wicked tormentors. But this extreme measure was carried into effect after Hill's rule had been fairly established.

Under his strict discipline everything worked fairly well at the start. But his too zealous eagerness to accomplish a reform led him to do what prudence and calm reason should have prevented. The following instance may serve as an example: Two women had set afloat some report concerning Hill, which, reaching his ears, he strongly resented. Immediate steps were taken to punish the offenders. A meeting was convened, consisting of the irate leader, his elders, sub-elders, and cadets, to pass judgment on the women. In the course of the meeting, they knelt for a few minutes while Hill prayed. Among the various petitions that he uttered, occurred this sentence: "If these women die the common death of all men, the Lord hath not sent me." The prayer ended, but there was no response. Not one present, with the exception of Hill himself, would pronounce the "amen." Nor was it to be expected that they would thus denounce the women who were nearly related to some of them. But their refusal to take part in the prayer enraged their leader still more, and, while he stood revealed before his followers in his true character, overzealous, revengeful, and tyrannical, the spell with which his influence had bound them was broken, and the hold he had obtained on the minds of some of them was forever lost.

Wrangling, quarreling, and abusive language were constantly kept up between the parties. Hill and his party, who were the stronger, caused the lives of the three other Englishmen to be daily embittered with hard treatment. Buffett in particular was forced to undergo severe punishment on account of a wrong done five or six years before Hill came. When Hill was informed of the matter, he considered it his duty to administer such penalty as would prove a wholesome lesson to Buffett in future. Nor would Nobbs have escaped were it not that at the time he was sick in bed, and Hill's cruelty did not quite reach to the extent of flogging a sick man. Nobbs, who was poetical, wrote a lively epigram on Hill, in the closing lines of which he mentioned the erection of the gallows—

"With a *Hill* to *enliven* the scene."

PITCAIRN AVENUE.

This at once met a retort, and thus the spirit of animosity was kept alive and never suffered to die.

The ill treatment to which the three Englishmen were constantly subjected at last reached a climax by their being forced to leave the island. Separated from their families, they were carried away on a schooner, the captain of which condemned Hill's doings unsparingly, while to the exiled men he showed the utmost kindness. They were taken to Tahiti, but did not remain there long, as an opportunity was soon afforded them of returning to the home of their adoption. Arriving there, they took their families with them and left, Nobbs and Evans going as far as the Gambier Islands, while Buffett went on to Tahiti.

When the cruel banishment had been effected, the men who before had yielded unquestioning obedience to Hill's orders, began to awake to the fact that they had been participating in a wholesale course of injustice and oppression. Their true friends had received ill usage at their hands, even unto banishment, while they had submitted to be ruled by a tyrant. Shame and remorse for the part they had taken, filled their minds, and they only waited the opportunity to have the exiles recalled.

It soon came. The captain of a schooner, the *Olivia*, making a call at the island at the time, was told all the facts of the case, and he very generously promised to go to the Gambier Islands and remove the two families of Nobbs and Evans to their home. This was accordingly done, and once more all were again on Pitcairn

Island, as Buffett and his family had arrived from Tahiti a short time before on the *Olive Branch*. While these last seemed to have gained in health during their sojourn at Tahiti, the two families who stayed at the Gambier Islands were extremely emaciated, owing to the poor food on which they were obliged to subsist. Their relatives and friends greeted them on their home coming with open arms, while expressions of affection and tears of joy, that spoke more than words, told how glad they were that all of them were permitted to meet again.

On the return of the exiled men, they found the island in an unsettled state. Divisions were rife among the people. Hill no longer exercised undisputed sway over their minds and actions. His power, once so great, was now quite broken. At this time there occurred a quarrel between Hill and one of his former elders, which narrowly escaped proving a very serious affair. The trouble arose in this way: A young girl, daughter of the ex-elder, had been charged with stealing some yams, and was proved guilty. The father was summoned before Hill, to hear what his daughter's sentence would be. Hill declared that the offender ought to be executed, or, at least, be made to suffer very severely for her fault. The father strongly opposed such harsh measures, and positively asserted that his daughter should not be subjected to the will of the merciless man. Aroused to fury by this opposition to his will, which the father steadily maintained, Hill rushed into his bedroom, and, grasping his sword, returned, and, waving it threateningly at his opponent, cried out, "Confess your sins, for you are a dead man." This he repeated with, if possible, increased fury, while his threatened victim, as he afterward declared, felt that his last hour had indeed come. A table stood between them, and young Quintall, although intimidated by the murderous fire that gleamed in Hill's eye, as well as by the sword that he was brandishing, quickly cleared the table at a bound, and, before Hill could divine his intention, laid a firm grip on the shoulders of his enemy, and by main force threw him upon the floor. Unable to do anything else but maintain his hold on his fallen foe, he was powerless to prevent the thrusts of Hill's sword. Fortunately, they resulted in a few slight scratches only, which were sufficiently deep, however, to leave lifelong scars on the breast of the intended victim. How long the struggle would have lasted had the combatants been left alone, it is not possible to say. A young man happened to pass by the house, and, catching a glimpse of what was passing within, took in the whole situation at once. Running as quickly as he could to his house, he soon returned armed with a musket, and called out that he was going to shoot Hill. Others, hearing the shout, came running together to learn what the cause of the disturbance was. Arriving at the scene of the quarrel, their first act was to dispossess Hill of his sword. He was then allowed to rise and retire peaceably to his room. Nothing further was done to him, but he did not receive his sword back again until the day when, friendless and unloved, he left the island forever.

Letters of complaint from the persecuted Buffett, Evans, and Nobbs had, in the meantime, been sent on to Valparaiso, asking redress from those who might and could render help and deliverance from Hill's power. In answer to their earnest appeal, the *Actæon* was sent to the island in 1836. She was commanded by Lord Edward Russell. His lordship, shortly after arriving, called a meeting, over which he himself presided. Permission was given to all concerned to speak their minds freely, a privilege of which each one readily availed himself. A warm and lively debate ensued, and while Hill was speaking in his own defense, one unruly member of the meeting would every now and again interrupt him with, "It's a lie, my lord," addressed to Lord Russell.

The proceedings of the court provoked much laughter, and all was greatly enjoyed by his lordship. One circumstance especially called forth peals of laughter. Hill was relating a story about a book that belonged to Hannah Young. Opposite to the motto "*Dieu et mon droit*," on the title-page, were written the following lines:—

> "God and my right we often see
>   Emblazoned abroad;
> Let them who read this motto be
>   With Jesus, right with God."

Beneath this Nobbs had placed his signature, "G. H. Nobbs, P. S. M." Hill had taken the liberty to add as a postscript this quotation from Holy Writ: "Alas, master! for it was borrowed." On Lord Russell's asking an explanation of the three initial letters subjoined to the name of Nobbs, Hill readily replied that *Nobbs* intended them to mean "Pastor and Spiritual Master," but, in *his* estimation, the correct rendering should be "Public Miscreant and Scoundrel." These lively thrusts were given by each party until his lordship declared that the whole proceeding was too good to finish at one sitting, and the meeting adjourned to the following day.

On the second day his lordship's decision was that Hill should be removed from the island as soon as possible, and the following year the *Imogen* arrived to carry that decision into effect. The first words spoken by her captain, when the boat from shore went off to the ship, were: "Is Joshua Hill still on the island? I am sent on purpose to remove him." The next day, at an early hour, Hill, with his few possessions, was conveyed on board the *Imogen*, where cold looks awaited him. Friendless and alone in the midst of strangers, the old man stood on the deck of the vessel that was to bear him away. With all his faults, aggravated as they were, it is impossible not to feel a deep sympathy in his hour of adversity for the poor old man, who, through a mistaken, perverted zeal, had rendered himself obnoxious to those whom he undoubtedly, and with all honesty of purpose, wished to benefit. Thus passed out of the history of Pitcairn Island Joshua Hill, whose memory is still freshly retained by those who knew him, rather as being associated with harshness, severity, and tyranny, than like that of the just, whose memory "smells sweet and blossoms in the dust."

THE FLAG OF OLD ENGLAND

CHAPTER VIII.

AFTER Mr. Hill's removal, Mr. Nobbs, with the hearty consent of nearly all the people, assumed sole charge as pastor and schoolmaster. Under his benign rule peace once more reigned, and the former brotherliness between the families, that had been so fully established under John Adams, was once more as fully resumed. While Mr. Nobbs devoted himself to the higher needs of the people, combining with his other duties those of a physician (to the best of his ability), Buffett had resumed his old trade of cabinet work, which he confined to such articles as workboxes, writing desks, and chests of drawers of all sizes. The wood of the *mero* tree, which the soil of the island abundantly produced, supplied all the material needed in the darker shades. The timber is exceedingly close grained and hard, and when fully matured becomes changed in color from dark red to

almost black, and takes polish beautifully. The bright
yellow color of the wood of the white-flower tree was
used for ornamenting, as it forms a pretty contrast
with the other. Buffett also instructed those among
the young men who showed any inclination to learn,
and was highly gratified at seeing them display
decided skill in the handiwork. John Evans, also,
who wished to try his hand at the trade, came with
the others to take lessons in practical work, and succeeded fairly well in the business.

Buffett, who was fond of a joke, used to relate how
one day, when he was at work in his house, Evans
came to him, bringing an unfinished workbox that
he was making, in his hand. Setting the box down,
he turned to Buffett, and began telling him how his
work was almost a failure, and was likely to come to
grief unless he obtained some much needed help from
the master hand. "In fact, Buffett," he said, "I just
came over to ask you to give it a licking." As soon
as Evans had finished speaking, Buffett, without a
word, took up the workbox, and, rapidly passing his
tongue over its smooth surface, set it down again, saying, with a hearty laugh, "There is your box; I have
given it a licking." Astonished beyond expression,
and indignant at having his request so literally fulfilled, Evans angrily snatched up the innocent cause
of the joke, and was hastening away, when Buffett
good-humoredly assured him that no offense was
intended, and he was at length prevailed on, though
reluctantly, to calm his ruffled feelings, and wait a few

minutes until Buffett had given the necessary help he asked for.

While Nobbs gave instruction to the children in the schoolroom, Buffett proposed to establish a class for young men, to give them instruction in navigation and the more advanced branches of arithmetic, and, in addition to these, studies upon such subjects of general information as they could obtain through the medium of books, though of these they had only a very limited supply. The more thoughtful among the young men eagerly availed themselves of even this chance of improvement, and organized themselves into a band, with Buffett at their head, who gave the name "Mutual Improvement Society" to their class. While it lasted, it was well attended, and most, if not all, of the members derived lasting benefit therefrom.

While Nobbs and Buffett were engaged in pursuits so congenial to them, the necessary cultivation of their allotments of land was performed by their wives and children, and whoever of their neighbors that would willingly assist. They themselves did but a trifling portion of the work. Evans, on the other hand, seemed to possess a natural liking for the soil and its cultivation, in which work he was aided by his strong and healthy wife.

It was now forty-seven years since the island had been settled, and in all that time no rules had been enacted for the government of the people. Conscience sometimes, and more frequently inclination, ruled them. But this state of things was about to be ended.

GROUP OF NATIVE MEN.

In the year 1838 Her Majesty's ship *Fly* came on a visit, and for the first time, to the evident satisfaction and pleasure of the islanders, the flag of Old England was hoisted on Pitcairn Island, Captain Elliott observing, "You are now under the protection of the English flag." From that time until the entire community was removed to Norfolk Island, they were annually visited by one or more of Her Majesty's ships of war.

Captain Elliott also strongly advised the people to have written laws by which they might be governed, and, further, to appoint a magistrate from among themselves to enforce those laws. Mr. Hill had also spoken strongly about the necessity and importance of such a step being taken, but his advice had not been acted upon. The captain's proposal was received differently, everybody being willing to carry out any plans that he thought would be best for them. Their unanimous choice fell upon the youngest son of Quintall, whose strong common sense and really excellent abilities recommended him as the fittest person to be nominated. When Hill first came among the people, Quintall attracted his particular notice, and Hill constituted him his chief elder. The two men possessed many similar traits of character, and on no point were they more agreed than in the intense dislike to the three other Englishmen. That Quintall could be a staunch friend was proved by the fact that he stood by Hill to the last, when everyone else had deserted him. In after years the intermarriages that took place between his own children and those of Nobbs and

Buffett were evident proofs that they did not share their father's prejudices.

Like Hill, he, too, when aroused by anger, was capable of committing deeds of cruelty, as the following story will show. Engaged in a dispute one day with John Evans, both men lost control over themselves, and began to abuse one another. The quarrel increased, and Quintall, being a powerful man, brought it to a termination by lifting Evans, who was small, as easily as he would a child, and throwing him violently into a pigsty, thereby causing him serious injury. This wicked act was recorded in the register of those times, for it was customary to enter therein every occurrence, however trivial, and whenever a case occurred which could not be satisfactorily adjusted by the local authorities, it was usual to postpone it until the arrival of a ship of war, to whose captain the matter was referred for decision. It was so in this case, but the fact that the perpetrator of the deed was at the time laid on his sick bed, from which he never again arose, prevented his receiving his just deserts, and so the passing of the sentence awaited a higher tribunal than that of earth.

A more pleasing theme than the story just related was the arrival of the first missionary vessel that ever called at the island. This was the *Camden*, which was sent out by the London Missionary Society. In her missionary visits to the various islands of the Pacific, she made a brief call at Pitcairn Island, having but one missionary on board, a Mr. Heath. The *Camden's*

stay extended only to four days, during which time Mr.
Heath gave two public addresses, and held several
meetings in Mr. Nobbs' house. Captain Morgan, who
commanded the vessel, also delivered an impressive
discourse from the text, "My son, give me thine heart."
A good supply of Bibles was left on the island, enough
for each family to have one. Captain Morgan also
sent out from England, on his arrival there, a box of
books, schoolbooks as well as religious publications,
and slates and pencils for the use of the school. These
were all thankfully received, as they supplied a very
pressing want, especially the last-named gifts.

In the year 1841 Christian's widow died. Her
name, given by the Englishmen, was Isabella, but as
Christian himself had dubbed her "Mainmast," this
latter name was the one by which she was exclusively
called, only it was abbreviated to "Mai'mas'." She
was of very advanced age when she died, but to the
last retained vivid recollections of the events of earlier
years, and used often to relate to her attentive listeners
the story of Captain Cook's visit to the Society Islands.
Once when he was in Tahiti he was suffering from a
severe attack of rheumatism. Some of the Tahitian
women took him in hand, and effected a cure by means
of the native remedy. This consisted of a preparation
of the *a'pi plant* (*arum gigantum*) which was externally
applied to the part or parts affected. The painful,
stinging properties of the plant (compared to which
the sting of the nettle is almost enjoyable) would seem
to lead one to decide in favor of the rheumatism, as

this remedy seems certainly worse than the disease.
But Mainmast declared that the dreadful remedy cured
Captain Cook. This old woman's death left but one
more remaining of the original party that came in
the *Bounty*, thus severing, link by link, the tie that
bound the younger portion of the community to those
who originally settled the colony.

Scarcely anything occurred to disturb the tranquil
round of life that the inhabitants enjoyed, and day
after day passed along in quiet monotony, broken only
by the arrival of some passing ship. The "event" of
every year was the visit of a man-of-war.

About the year 1847 an accident befell Mr. Nobbs'
eldest son, which nearly proved fatal. He, in company
with some other young men, had one day gone out to
hunt goats. As they were returning home, Reuben
Nobbs slipped and fell. The loaded gun he carried was
instantly discharged, most of its contents being lodged
in his right hip, while the ball passed entirely through.
He was brought home, and his father attended him.
Month after month passed, and, although he did not
grow worse there still was no perceptible improvement. When the next man-of-war came, the *Spy*, her
surgeon examined the wound, and, probing it, ex-
tracted large pieces of wadding, the presence of which
had prevented recovery. After that the cure was
rapid, and the young man was soon able to walk with
the help of a crutch. But the result was a lameness
that unfitted him for such work as life on the island
required, and, as he had good business abilities, his

father, who had friends in Valparaiso, wrote to them asking if they would kindly obtain for his son some means of gaining a living. The answer was favorable, and in due time Reuben Nobbs arrived at Valparaiso, to begin his duties as clerk in a commercial establishment. He was cordially received, and, by a diligent application to work, and the determination to please his employers, he succeeded not only in learning to do that which was required of him, but also in giving entire satisfaction to his employers during his whole stay.

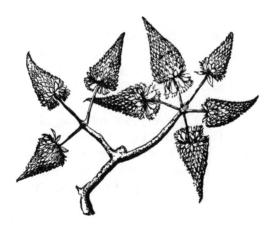

CHAPTER IX.

HE year 1848 is remembered as the first year when the 24th of May, the Queen's birthday, was kept as a holiday. The young men, with Mr. Nobbs at their head, started the celebration. The *Bounty's* old gun was made to do duty on the occasion in firing a salute in honor of Her Majesty, and every old musket that could be put to such a use, with as heavy charges as could be carried, was pressed into service to assist the *Bounty's* gun in making all the noise possible. The one bell on the island was kept ringing merrily, while, to add to the other sounds, cheer after cheer rang from the throats of the whole community, who had assembled to show loyalty to their sovereign.

The bell was a gift presented to the islanders in 1844 by the people on board the *Basilisk*, man-of-war, to be used for calling the worshipers to church. For years a bugle horn had been used for this purpose, and when that wore out, a musket took its place, one shot being fired as the hour for divine service approached. The musket was in use at the time of the *Basilisk's* visit. The beautiful, deep-toned bell, that was so thoroughly appreciated, at once displaced the discordant old musket, but never had it rung so merrily, nor so long, as when it lent its aid to celebrate the Queen's birthday.

But, with all the noise they were able to produce, they felt that something important was lacking. They had no song suitable for the great occasion. The national anthem was then unknown, and what were they to do in this dilemma? Fortunately, the question did not long remain unanswered. The loyal-hearted and enthusiastic Mr. Nobbs proved himself equal to the occasion. A song was quickly composed, and heartily, if not harmoniously, sung by the untrained voices of the islanders, to the tune of "The Girl I Left behind Me." The concluding stanza—

> "We'll fire the gun, the *Bounty's* gun,
>   And set the bell a-ringing,
>   And give three cheers for England's Queen,
>   And three for Pitcairn's Island,"

was followed by a succession of ringing cheers, repeated until the hills echoed again with the sound.

The memory of that day, with all its noise and merriment, and the simple pleasures that were so thoroughly enjoyed, was kept fresh in the minds of the women, who determined not to be outdone by the men.   Accordingly, they made what preparations they could for their celebration, when the day came around again.

Let me tell you first something about the dress of the women of that period. They no longer wore exclusively, Sundays as well as week days, the homely frock gathered into a band around the throat, and beneath this frock a scant petticoat such as had been worn since they had known the use of the needle. Gradually, gowns, long waisted and bone ribbed, after the patterns sent on shore by ship captains' wives, and also from time to time sent to the island by friends in England and elsewhere, took the place, for Sunday wear, of the primitive frock that had been worn so long.

Every woman's ambition was to possess a gown, and, notwithstanding the difficulties attending the cutting and fitting, each one was supplied, the more elderly women wearing a pattern differing somewhat from that which the younger women wore. Mr. Nobbs did what he could to advance the tastes of the women in regard to dress, and upon his wife devolved the dreadful task of cutting and fitting, made thus dreadful because there was no previous knowledge of the art; and several days would elapse before even one garment would be ready for the needle. Fortunately, some of the younger women were quick to learn, and, in spite of limited advantages, they were soon able to take the burden from Mrs. Nobbs' hands. Occasionally help was given them by some of the ship captains

THE ISLAND SAWMILL.

wives that visited the island. Knitting was also taught by them, but soon became a lost art.

On the Queen's birthday in question, the matrons and maidens decided to dress in their best—white gowns preferred—and spend the day as their fancy led them. One old grandmother proposed that a knot of white ribbon be worn on the left shoulder, which was done, strips of cloth supplying the place of ribbons. When the twenty-fourth day of May arrived, cloudless and beautiful, it was greeted with loud and loyal cheers from all, while the women and girls rose with the dawn to array themselves in honor of the day, and surprise their husbands and brothers, fathers and lovers, with their display, as all their preparations had been kept secret.

The men were invited to come and join in the merry-making, and they obeyed with alacrity. All work was laid aside, and everyone entered heartily into the sports and games that followed. The older women attended to the babies and prepared the early supper, the materials for which had been supplied beforehand. After the plentiful repast, all were at liberty to enjoy themselves as they pleased. The daughters of the mutineers, being now themselves the grandmothers, entered with zest into the sports, and contributed not a little to the general entertainment by reviving many of the games learned from their Tahitian mothers.

They introduced into their games and sports the beating of calabashes with sticks, performed with extreme precision, to which the players kept time, moving with noiseless step and an easy grace that was pleasing to witness. This performance was called the *ihara*. Another native dance, the *uri*, was performed by Susannah, the girl of fifteen who came in the *Bounty*, now an old woman of seventy-four, and blind in one eye. She displayed remarkable liveliness in honor of the Queen's birthday, and her performance provoked mirth from the younger people, who had never seen the dance before. This old woman died in the September following, 1850, at the age of seventy-five, being the last survivor of those who came to the island from Tahiti sixty years before.

The merry players kept up the dancing to a late hour. What mattered if most of them danced with bare feet; that did not affect their light-heartedness and happiness. A drum and tambourine supplied all the music they wanted. The island boasted one fiddle, but no one considered himself sufficiently expert in the use of the bow to volunteer his services. At last the simple enjoyments of the day ended, only to linger in the memory as a bright and pleasing recollection.

The singing of the islanders had been improved as the years passed. When John Adams had the sole care of the young community, he did not neglect entirely the training of their voices, although the result was not all that could be wished. He succeeded in impressing on their memories one simple and plaintive air, which, slightly modified, was made to suit either common, short, or long meter. This was the only attempt at singing made by the islanders until Buffett

came amongst them. The ninety-fifth psalm of Watts'
Version was a great favorite among the people, and
that to which John Adams' tune was oftenest sung.*
Buffett soon sought to introduce at least a change of
tunes into the services of the church, and, being gifted
with a good voice, he managed, with the help of an
accordion, to lead the people a few steps further on.
A book of church music given him at Tahiti supplied
a variety of tunes, but nothing more was attempted
than the simple air. Nor were the tunes sung in uni-
son, as the following incident will show.

In the earlier part of 1850 a ship touched at the island
on her way to California. Five gentlemen, four of
whom were passengers, came on shore. The fifth was
the supercargo of the vessel. The day following was
Sunday, and the visitors attended service in the little
church with the islanders, Mr. Nobbs officiating as
pastor, while John Buffett led the singing. If the
visitors expected to derive pleasure from that most
delightful part of public worship, they were disap-

---

*It was a custom wi'l .ne three daughters of John Adams, even until
advanced age, to meet together, and read a portion of God's word. They
would unfailingly close their devotions by singing the tune their father taught
them. A stanza from the second psalm, which they always sang, found in the
Scottish Bibles, seems peculiarly associated with the plaintive air. ·It is as fo
lows: –

> "A sure decree I will declare,—
> The Lord has said to me,
> 'Thou art my only Son; this day
> Have I begotten thee.'"

On his first visit to Norfolk Island, and at his special request, the three old
ladies sang the above to the late and much-loved Bishop Selwyn, their pleasant
acquiescence and unaffected, simple manners winning for them the admiration
and esteem of the good bishop and his lady.

pointed. The effect produced by the congregation, singing without regard to time or tune, was so discordant and jarring that Mr. Carleton, the supercargo, declared that the sounds grating upon his ears nearly compelled him to take his hat and leave the house.

The next day, Monday, the ship was seen at a long distance from the island, but. thinking that the captain would certainly return for his passengers, no apprehensions were entertained that they would be left behind. But so it proved, and the only explanation that could be given of the captain's conduct was that the wind, which was favorable, was steadily increasing, and he did not want to lose it. He left his passengers to the hospitality of the islanders, and the kind favor of the first captain that should call going the same way, and took away with him one of the islanders who was on board when the ship sailed. This man went to California and returned by way of Sydney.

When the surprised and forsaken passengers had ascertained that they had been left behind, they wisely decided to make the best of the circumstances. Mr. Carleton, who was highly gifted with musical talent, mentioned to John Buffett the matter of trying to mprove the singing of the people. In reply he was requested to undertake the task. This he at first declined, saying that he would not have the time he should require to produce anything like a satisfactory result, and so would rather not attempt it. However, as no opportunity came within the week for him to leave the island, he finally yielded to Buffett's earnest and oft-repeated requests, and consented to make a beginning.

He invited all who were willing to come, to meet every evening at one of the houses, and from among them he chose such as seemed to possess some musical ability. These he instructed particularly, that they might be able to carry forward the work. The pleasing results produced by harmony of sounds served to awaken in the hearts of the learners such eagerness and anxiety to do their best as to greatly encourage their teacher in his efforts. With the determination to succeed, it was not very surprising that in the short space of one week they accomplished a result beyond their highest hopes, and when Mr. Carleton took his departure the second week after, it was in full confidence that the important work which had so well begun, would not be left to stagnate. Nor was he mistaken. An old man used to tell how he was affected by the first sounds of harmony that he heard. He said: "The first tune I listened to was Devizes. Buffett was singing the air, and Mr. Carleton the bass. I stood by open mouthed, drinking in the sweet sounds, and thinking it must be like heaven."

When Mr. Carleton left the island, he was accompanied by Mr. Brodie, one of the four passengers, who pleaded that the captain should take him, instead of any of the others, as there were accommodations on the ship for only two. This gentlemen afterward wrote an interesting account of the island, which he published. Baron de Thierry, one of the remaining three, continued the work begun by Mr. Carleton. He attempted to teach drawing also, but without success, possibly because the fingers of his pupils, having from earliest childhood been trained to use the hoe and to manage the wheelbarrow, could not be made to hold and carry the pencil. The baron one night when Mr. Carleton was engaged in teaching his singing class, caused the singing to give place to a hearty burst of merriment. One of the pupils, with her strong, clear voice, was ascending the scale, and as she arose to the highest notes without any apparent effort, enunciating every syllable clearly and distinctly, the baron called out: "Stop, stop. No one but my daughter is able to do it like that."

The enforced stay of the five gentlemen on Pitcairn Island was productive of one of the best and most satisfactory results, for all the subsequent pleasure and delight that the people, both of Pitcairn Island and Norfolk Island, derive from music, instrumental as well as vocal, had their origin in those early lessons taught by Mr. Carleton. The memory of this man is revered and loved among the people, who owe to him so much of the pleasure they receive from this high and ennobling art.

VISIT of H·M·S· PORTLAND

CHAPTER X.

THE time was now drawing near when an important change was to take place in the history of the Pitcairn islanders. Ever since it had been arranged that the island should be visited yearly by a British ship of war, its arrival was the looked-for event of each year. When Admiral Sir Fairfax Moresby was commander in chief on the Pacific station, an officer on board one of Her Majesty's ships, while on a visit to the island, proposed that the women send a request to the admiral to pay them a visit. A letter was written forthwith, and signed by several of the island matrons and maidens. The admiral was pleased to respond to the letter in person, and arrived at the island in August, 1852, in his flagship, the *Portland*. His coming was greeted by the people with every demonstration of joy, which reached its height when, gathered beneath a grove of orange trees, they listened to the band that the admiral had kindly ordered ashore, and enjoyed such delicious strains of music as they never had dreamed of. From the admiral down to the humblest seaman, everybody on board the *Portland* showed kindness to the islanders, so much so that the visits of the *Portland* were considered by the people as comprising the golden period in their island's history. The admiral was accompanied by two of his sons, the younger of whom, Mr. Fortescue Moresby, by his pleasant, cheerful ways and winning manners, endeared himself greatly to the hearts of the islanders.

Among the earliest subjects that engaged Admiral Moresby's attention was the position of Mr. Nobbs as an unordained pastor of the people, and he took on himself the responsibility of sending that gentleman to England, with a letter of recommendation to the bishop of London, requesting him to receive Mr. Nobbs as a candidate for ordination, adding that his faithful services to the people of his adopted home, and the good that he had been the means of accomplishing, might be considered in place of whatever deficiency there was in his theological training.

When the *Portland* left Pitcairn Island, Mr. Nobbs left too, accompanied by one of his daughters, Miss Jane Nobbs, who went as far as Valparaiso, where her brother Reuben was. Here she was received by a very worthy family, who showed her every consideration and kindness. Before Mr. Nobbs could consent to leave his flock, it was arranged that the *Portland's*

PARLIAMENT OF PITCAIRN ISLAND.

chaplain, Mr. Holman, should remain behind and supply the place of the absent pastor.   A lad from the
Portland also remained with Mr. Holman.   The people on the whole regarded it as a very satisfactory
arrangement, although no one could quite fill the place
Mr. Nobbs had so long and so ably filled.

Arriving at Valparaiso, Mr. Nobbs took passage on
the steamer *Orinoco* to England, which place he safely
reached, and was duly ordained.   The late Prince
Consort honored him with an interview, and he had
also a glimpse of the Queen.   Indeed, Her Majesty,
in passing, extended to him her royal hand, which he
warmly grasped, and heartily shook, after which she
quietly, and without a word, passed on.   This little
incident was often recalled by the worthy man, and
always with some degree of amusement at the possible mistake he made at the time.   In Mr. Nobbs
interview with his Royal Highness, the Prince showed
much kindly interest in his far-distant home, and made
many inquiries respecting his labors there.   A salary
of £50 a year was granted him, and, had there been
proof that Mr. Nobbs had indeed been promoted to
the rank of lieutenant in the naval service, another
fifty would have been added.   His stay in England
was too short to admit of his accepting many of the
numerous invitations given him by persons of rank
and wealth, but in one particular case he never ceased
to regret that circumstances made it impossible for
him to attend.   This was an invitation to call on
Messrs. Wilson and Cook, gentlemen who had sent

8

large gifts of useful household articles to Pitcairn Island a short time before. In May, 1853, Mr. Nobbs reached home again, the whole time of his absence not extending over nine months.

One very sad and fatal accident had happened during his absence. When the *Portland* reached Valparaiso, Admiral Moresby sent the *Virago* on to Pitcairn Island, that the people might see a steamship for the first time. She came in the month of January, near its close. On the day that she was to leave, almost everybody was on board, and the vessel had steamed around the little island, much to the wonder and delight of the people. It was toward the close of the day, and when the people were about to return on shore, that a farewell salute from the *Bounty's* gun was to be fired. Among those who were attending to the gun was the magistrate, Matthew McCoy. The ramrod used on the occasion was an old, smoothly-planed rafter made from the wood of the cocoanut tree, very hard, and which had been used in building. Unknown to those in attendance was a nail in the rafter. This, coming in contact with the gun, already heated by the sun, caused the powder to ignite before all was ready. In an instant the gun was discharged, and the men attending it were scattered in all directions, several feet from the spot.

The untimely discharge soon brought a small crowd of the people left on shore to the scene of the accident, and, as the disaster was witnessed from the *Virago*, the boats were quickly got ready, and as soon as possible the doctor and his assistants were at the place.   Two young men, William Evans and Driver Christian, were severely wounded, but Matthew Mc-Coy had received his death blow.   His right arm was fearfully shattered, and he was, besides, much bruised and injured.   The arm was amputated, in the hope that his life might be spared, but all that surgical skill could do was of no avail, for during the night of January 27, 1853, he died.   Thus ended, in sadness and gloom, the day that had dawned so brightly, and which had been so greatly enjoyed by all.   The dead man was buried with funeral honors, all the officers and men that could be spared from the *Virago* being present.   But no outward display could allay the sorrow or calm the grief of the desolate widow and fatherless children, who so deeply mourned their irreparable loss.   Before the *Virago* sailed, the *Bounty's* gun was spiked to prevent it from ever being used again.   After having lain and rusted for nearly forty years, it was at length used as the foundation for a flagstaff.

As stated above, Mr. Nobbs reached home in May and immediately resumed his duties as pastor, the people observing that he seemed to have acquired a somewhat more dignified bearing after having been ordained, although his thorough kindliness of disposition and interest in everything that concerned the people's welfare, remained unchanged.

The arrival of the *Portland* was most timely, as the people were suffering from the effects of a severe drought, and were obliged to subsist on whatever they could get, unripe pumpkins forming their principal diet. Liberal supplies from the ship's stores provided them with sufficient food to last until better times appeared. The admiral then left, taking with him Mr. Holman and the lad that had remained with him. The *Portland* proceeded on her way to the Gambier Islands, but soon returned, going on to Valparaiso. As she came near enough to Pitcairn Island for the people to communicate by signals, one of distress was hoisted, for the islanders, almost without an exception, were suffering greatly from an attack of influenza. Misinterpreting the signal, the *Portland* kept on, but was stopped when a boat was seen putting off from the land, manned by a few poor fellows, who were hardly able to manage their oars. On learning the cause of their coming, the admiral and his officers at once went on shore, and the report of the men was confirmed by the sight of the pitiable condition of the islanders.

Everything that kindness could suggest was done for the sufferers, all the visitors doing what they could to relieve the distress around them; nor did they take their final leave of the island until there were visible signs of improvement. So attached had all the islanders become to the people on the ship that much real sorrow was felt at parting; indeed, the leave taking was such that men, as well as women and children, wept freely, as they looked their last on the faces of the kind friends who had done so much for them, and who were not ashamed to mingle their tears with the tears of those they were leaving behind. The blessings of a grateful people followed their departing visitors.

Reuben Nobbs, who had accompanied his father and sister home from Valparaiso, remained with his family for a few months; but, on the arrival of H. M. S. *Dido*, in the following year, he prepared to return to his duties at Valparaiso on that ship. But his stay was short, and he was soon home again, as consumption had made rapid progress. Kind and willing hands carried him from the place where he was landed, for he was universally beloved, and conveyed him to his home, where he lingered on until March 2, 1855, when he died.

Two accidents, each fatal in its nature, happened shortly after this. The first death was the result of a wound in the foot of a lad, caused by the barbed point of an arrow made of iron. Lockjaw set in, and after the terrible agonies that followed, he died. The other accident was sudden, and death was instantaneous. It was on a Saturday, and most of the men were out in their canoes fishing. A young man named Daniel McCoy, with his wife, went to the northwest side of the island, at a place called the Lookout, to fish among the rocks. Several other young people went in the same direction, but separated themselves into different parties to fish.

Dan and his wife went alone to a spot to reach which they must either swim a narrow passage of water, or climb a few steps, and then descend a steep and very dangerous path among the rocks. They chose the latter, and in making the descent the young man lost his hold, slipped, and fell. The fall was not high, scarcely ten feet; but he fell heavily and broke his back. With one dreadful groan, and a last dying look upon his wife, he immediately expired. Almost distracted, she went in search of their companions, who were at some distance from them, fishing. Grief and horror seemed to lend wings to her speed, as she passed over the rough stones and jagged rocks that for the most part formed her pathway. Only a few minutes sufficed for her to reach a spot where she could see her companions, and make them understand by signs that their assistance was required. The frantic cries and wild gesticulations at once convinced them that something dreadful had occurred, and they instantly started to learn what had happened.

It was soon told, and, while some of the fishing party returned with the bereaved wife to the scene of the awful accident, others hastened home to tell the sad news, and to get assistance to carry the body home. As nearly all the men were out fishing, these had to be summoned by means of signals, and as soon as possible a whaleboat was launched to go on the sad errand. In a short time the scarcely cold, lifeless burden was tenderly placed within, and taken back to the home whence, but a few hours before, he had left in all the strength and pride of young manhood Scarcely anything noteworthy occurred during the twelve months that followed the death of Daniel McCoy, which took place on the seventh day of April, 1855. Life gradually assumed its ordinary, monotonous round; but every day was bringing nearer the day when everything was to be changed.

REMOVAL TO NORFOLK ISLAND

CHAPTER XI.

WHEN, in 1853, Admiral Moresby visited Pitcairn Island, he saw that the rapidly increasing numbers of the inhabitants would soon necessitate a removal of a part, or the whole, of the community to a larger place, although he judged that Pitcairn Island, if brought under proper cultivation, was capable of maintaining a thousand inhabitants. The admiral argued that as a removal must be made at some future time, it would be the wisest course to have it done as early as possible, only he stipulated that all the people should go together.

And now the time was rapidly approaching. A report was sent to the home government concerning the matter, and early in the year 1856 H. M. S. *Juno* was sent from the colonies to inform the islanders that arrangements were being made for their removal to a larger island, and also to advise them to make the necessary preparations for their departure.

The tidings were received with different feelings. Some were ready to seize the opportunity of improving their worldly prospects, and the very thought of a change from their hitherto quiet lives was hailed with delight, while others, to whom home and its associations were dearer than any prospect that could be held out to them, preferred to remain, and probably were only restrained from so doing because the advice of their good friend, the admiral, was that all should go and receive their grant of land.

The island chosen for the future home of the Pitcairn islanders was Norfolk Island, once a penal settlement. The island is about twenty miles in circumference, and well capable of maintaining several thousand inhabitants.

In the latter part of April, 1856, the *Morayshire*, commanded by Captain Joseph Mathers, arrived from Sydney, to carry the emigrants to their new home. By the second day of May everything was ready, and the time had come to say farewell to the dear old spot where all their lives had been spent. Some, with buoyant hopes and bright expectations, stepped on board the ship that was to carry them away, while others—and these the far greater number—with sad hearts and tear-dimmed eyes left their island home. Utterly lonely and desolate, the little rock stood in the vast ocean as it slowly receded from view, and many a silent tear was shed and final farewell whispered for

the dear old home that most of them were to behold
no more, and which to many was most sacred because
of the loved ones sleeping there.

The passage to Norfolk Island was accomplished in
thirty-six days, and was, on the whole, rather pleasant
than otherwise to the emigrants. But few of them suffered from seasickness during the entire voyage. On the
8th of June, 1856, the *Morayshire* arrived at Norfolk
Island, and well pleased was the worthy captain to get
rid of the noisy crowd, the children more especially,
who tried his patience sorely, and who often enlivened
the ship with their cries and screams. No death occurred on the passage, but one poor little baby who
was sick all the way, lingered only a few days after
landing, and then died.

When the *Morayshire* arrived at Norfolk Island, H.
M. S. *Herald* was already there surveying. Boats
from the latter ship boarded the new arrival, bringing
acceptable supplies of fresh provisions. Her people
also very kindly assisted in landing the emigrants and
their goods. The crew of a whaling vessel rendered
help as well. When the *Morayshire* left, after a stay
of a little over two weeks, the captain took away the
few persons that had been on the island to take care
of the property ere it passed into other hands. The
passengers who left Norfolk Island on the *Morayshire*
were a Mr. Stuart, who acted as governor, and his wife,
a man by the name of Rogers, his wife and little
daughter, and an elderly couple named Waterson.
Besides these were eight reformed convicts, whose
work was to look after the affairs of the place.

Old Mrs. Waterson related a dream that made an impression upon her mind. A few nights before the emigrants landed, she seemed to see a woman, tall, large, and dark complexioned, standing by her side. So vivid was everything connected with the dream, even to the woman's name, Rachel, that she felt convinced that the person was on the coming ship. Accordingly, when the people landed, she started off in search of the reality, and scanned with curious eagerness each face that she saw. Not meeting on the street anyone that answered to the description, she went on toward the pier, and, within a few minutes' walk of the place, discovered the object of her search sitting on the steps of the Convicts' Hospital. A warm welcome and greeting followed, with the explanation that the acquaintance had been already made in a dream, and Mrs. Waterson was especially gratified to learn that the dream was true to the very name, the person being Rachel Evans, the daughter of John Adams. Even before the old lady left the island, the pleasing acquaintance had ripened into warm friendship.

Rogers' occupation on the island was that of a stock keeper and overseer. Walking along a certain road one day, in company with some of the recent settlers, he observed, in a playful spirit, that when that particular road was being made, he was among the gang of convicts so employed, having been sent to Norfolk Island on the charge of striking down his superior officer. "But," he remarked pleasantly, "my term of punishment expired some time ago." Seven other men, ex-convicts nearly all, made up the total of those who remained to look after the place. These men attended to the live stock, milked the cows, kept the dairy, and performed such work. The kindness and attention shown by every one of them to the newcomers could not be surpassed.

Each one exerted himself in pointing out to the new arrivals the different buildings and their various uses, among them the old and new barracks, the government house, the jail and prison, all strongly built of stone, some of which were beautiful as well as strong. Many dreadful tales were also told concerning the island and those who were sent there to be punished, but scarcely a trace remained to testify to the truth of the dark stories of blood and crime. At one place, outside of the burying ground, was shown a mound several feet in length, where moldered the dust of thirteen men who were hung for some dreadful crime on the trees above, while their open grave yawned beneath them.

An eyewitness related how, one day, when a gang of convicts was constructing a bridge over a stream, one of them murdered a constable who was in charge of the gang. From this dreadful act the scene of the murder received its name, and the "Bloody Bridge" stands, a lasting monument of the awful crime committed there. A tragic story was told of a convict who contrived to make his escape from Norfolk Island to another small island some three miles distant, called Philip Island. By some means this man, known as

GROUP OF NATIVE CHILDREN.

Jacky-Jacky, was discovered, and a boat was immediately dispatched to secure the escaped prisoner. Finding himself discovered and pursued, and choosing death rather than capture, Jacky-Jacky started to the highest point of the island, several hundred feet above the sea level, where he cast himself off and so perished.

These were only some of the stories that were told by those who were themselves witnesses of the awful scenes, stories still more dark and fearful in their nature than were those in connection with the early settlement of the island lately deserted by the emigrants. But the deeds of horror and bloodshed had passed away with the lives of those who committed them, and everything betokened calmness and peace when the little colony entered on their newly granted possession.

A GOODLY HERITAGE

CHAPTER XII.

NORFOLK ISLAND, henceforth to become the home of the Pitcairn islanders, possesses remarkable beauty. Having all their lives been accustomed to wooden houses of the plainest description, roofed with thatch, and standing here and there embosomed amid trees, the sight of regularly laid out streets and stone-built houses was an entirely new experience to the new settlers. When they took possession of their present home, all the dwelling houses, as well as the government buildings, were in a good state of preservation, and some of the latter were splendid structures.

The government house occupied a conspicuous place on a slight eminence nearly in the center of the town, and its spacious apartments, as well as its exterior, were well kept. The large garden adjoining showed signs of former care, but everything had been allowed to run wild, and the grapevines mingled in

(126)

happy confusion with the honeysuckle, nasturtium, and other flowering creepers.

Inclosed within high stone walls were the buildings of the old and new barracks, while near to the latter stood the ruins of what had been a fine hospital, which a fire had destroyed. Next to this, but separated by a wall, was the handsome commissariat store—now the church of the present inhabitants.

The large, gloomy prison was the central figure in a group of buildings that stood near the sea, having the Protestant church on one side, and the Roman Catholic chapel on the other. This still retained many signs of the outward services of the latter church, notably the gaudy pictures that ornamented the walls, a large one being that of the virgin and child.

Separated from these churches by a narrow, sunless passage, formed by the surrounding walls, were the jail buildings, strongly built of stone. Of special interest was the place where the gallows used to be erected when death was the penalty for crime. Although the time had gone by forever when such scenes could be witnessed, a feeling akin to horror could not be suppressed when passing beneath the spot where so many had taken their last farewell of life, and the silent, narrow cells around seemed almost in the echo of one's footfall to give forth the sad sighs and groans of despair, as the condemned criminal awaited the moment when he should be called forth to meet his doom.

Until a more settled state of things was reached, on

9

their immediate arrival the families were arranged into groups of two and three, and messed together. Two women, whose respective families occupied the same house, went out one day in search of green herbs for food. They congratulated themselves on finding a good supply of onions, and brought their treasures home, pleased at the thought of the relish they would add to the evening meal. A hearty laugh greeted the discovery that their precious onions were the bulbs of the narcissus, which in their ignorance they had so naturally mistaken for onions.

The dwelling houses differed in every respect from, and were altogether superior to, the thatched cottages that the people had so lately occupied. These were built mostly of stone, the walls within being neatly plastered, and they were roofed with shingles, supplied from the Norfolk Island pine. The houses generally consisted of four large rooms with chimneys attached. Each kitchen, which was a separate building, was floored with stone, and had a spacious fireplace and a brick oven on one side of the chimney. The interior was made light and clean by being frequently whitewashed. Attached to each cottage was a garden; and flowers fair and fragrant delighted the senses of both sight and smell. Altogether the change was a decided gain, and everything bespoke only prosperity and happiness in store for the people that had been so highly favored.

To the Pitcairn islanders Norfolk Island was literally a land "flowing with milk and honey." Although the

THE "PITCAIRN" AND MAN-OF-WAR OFF PITCAIRN ISLAND.

sight of a cow was a familiar one to them, they were
scarcely prepared for the large numbers of strong,
healthy cattle that they saw, which supplied the milk,
while honey was obtained from the hollow trees
where the wild bees built their hives. The island, too,
supported some two or three thousand sheep, besides
cattle and horses; but the sheep were not entirely
free from disease, and many of them died. The grass
that covered a large portion of the island afforded
abundant pasture for the flocks and herds that fed
there.

The soil and climate of the island were favorable
for the cultivation of various fruits, and lemons, guavas,
peaches, figs, white and purple grapes, loquats,
quinces, mulberries, pomegranates, watermelons, etc.,
etc., were produced in great abundance.

The island was well wooded. Extensive groves of
the Norfolk Island pine lent their aid to delight the
eye, while a variety of noble trees beautified and en-
riched the land, their luxuriant foliage affording a
pleasing shade for the feathered songsters that awoke
the echoes so sweetly with their warbling notes.

Streams of water traverse the island in several directions, while not infrequently the water is hid from
view by the thick growth of flags and reeds that cover
their marshy banks, and the streams themselves teem
with eel life. The abundant supply of water was by
no means the least of the blessings that had been
bestowed upon the people, for in their old home they
had known what it was to suffer for want of water.

But now "the lines were fallen unto them in pleasant places; yea, they had a goodly heritage."   Indeed, so fair was that heritage that it seemed impossible to realize that it was ever the abode of so much misery and crime; and the words of the Christain poet could not have been more aptly applied than to this lovely island,

> "Where every prospect pleases,
> And only *man* is vile."

Along the southern shore stretches a long line of coral reef, and this, extending some distance into the sea, renders it unsafe for a ship to approach too near the land.   A little beyond this reef stands a rock known as Nepean Island, only relieved from utter barrenness by one or two pine trees.   On this rock the whale birds congregate in great numbers to deposit their eggs, which are eagerly sought for by the people for food.   While Nepean Island is covered with sea birds in their laying season, Philip Island, which stands further seaward, is overrun with wild rabbits, that make their home there and feed on the scanty herbage that the poor soil produces.   Excellent fish of many varieties abound in the waters around the island.   Surrounded with all that they needed, and still living together in one unbroken circle, everything seemed to promise contentment and happiness.   But, as will be seen, it was not long before the hearts of some pined for the old home, and desired to return.

About two months after the new settlers had arrived, the bishop of New Zealand visited Norfolk Island in his yacht *Southern Cross*, bringing a large supply of

flour and other necessary things for the people's immediate wants.   He had come to the island a short time
before, but as the *Morayshire* had not yet arrived, had
returned to New Zealand.   Now, on this second trip,
he had brought his lady with him, and also his chaplain, the Rev. J. C. Patteson, who was destined to
become a martyr to the cause he loved.

Mrs. Selwyn remained on Norfolk Island, while the
bishop went back to his labors.   She soon won the
hearts of the people, and gave much assistance in
teaching in the day school as well as in the Sunday
school.   She tried to impress upon the minds of the
young women and girls whom she taught, the importance of practicing habits of cleanliness and industry
while young, teaching them also how to cook.   This
energetic lady was not satisfied with merely giving
instruction, but would frequently visit her scholars at
their homes to see whether those instructions had been
followed or not.   In this way more lasting good was
accomplished, and much real benefit resulted from her
patient and conscientious labors.

When the Pitcairn islanders first came into posses·
sion of Norfolk Island, they understood that the island
belonged to them, for so had they interpreted the letter
sent them before their removal, by Sir William Denison, the governor at that time of New South Wales.
On arriving at their new home they found that two
men were already there to divide the land among the
new arrivals.   These latter quietly informed them that
their services were not needed, as the islanders were

able to manage for themselves.   The two men left on the *Morayshire*, and, having reported to the proper authorities, two other surveyors were promptly dispatched to Norfolk Island with orders to measure the entire island and divide it into fifty-acre lots.   Each family had fifty acres to a share, a rather smaller portion than they had at first shared out among themselves.   Subsequently, when the governor himself visited the island, his letter was shown him as sufficient authority to justify the people in the course they had taken.   This document he calmly got possession of, and remarked something to the effect that matters were somewhat changed since the letter was penned.*

On Sir William's next visit to Norfolk Island he informed the people that a schoolmaster and a miller with their families were then on their way from England to settle amongst them.   There were, besides, a shoemaker and a stone mason.   "But," added the gov-

---

*The possession of Norfolk Island was a much-mooted question.   When Bishop Selwyn was in charge of New Zealand as his diocese, it was his wish to remove the headquarters of the Melanesian Mission to Norfolk Island, but neither the Pitcairn Island committee at home, nor the governor of New South Wales, Sir W. Denison, deemed it best that it should be so   Some few years later, when Bishop Patteson was head of the mission, the matter was again brought up   While some of the people were in favor of the movement, others strongly opposed it, but the matter was finally settled by the bishop's purchasing several thousand acres of land, being granted permission to do so by Sir John Young, governor of New South Wales, he having been so authorized by the home government   Thus was the desire of Bishop Selwyn's heart fulfilled in the removal of the Melanesian Mission from New Zealand to Norfolk Island.

When His Excellency Lord Augustus Loftus made an official visit to Norfolk Island in 1884, he sought to remove the impression "tenaciously held" by the people that the island was entirely theirs, and spoke very plainly to them respecting the use and abuse of the island, dwelling strongly on the fact that so many trees should be suffered to be cut down without planting others in their stead.

ernor, "I stopped the shoemaker in Sydney, for I did not like the looks of the man."

A letter had been written to the people about this time by their old friend the Baron de Thierry, then residing in Auckland. It contained such sound advice and good counsel to the people respecting their right use of the many privileges accorded them, that Sir William declared it "worthy a place in the archives of the island" The governor himself gave much wise counsel to the people, and encouraged them to exert themselves to the best of their ability in the discharge of their several duties in the untried life that lay before them, showing how much depended upon their own efforts to insure success in the general improvement of themselves and their surroundings.

In due time the expected party from England arrived. The school, which was then kept by Simon Young, was immediately given into the hands of Mr. Thomas Rossiter. He was an excellent disciplinarian, and proved himself fully qualified to assume the task of managing and controlling the children, who often tried his patience. One of the spacious rooms on the second floor of the new barracks had been converted into a schoolroom, and here, once every week, Mr. Nobbs, for several years, was in the habit of visiting the children for the purpose of giving some religious instruction. This consisted principally in thoroughly grounding them in the teachings of the church catechism, and putting the more advanced pupils through a series of questions and answers preparatory to their becoming candidates for confirmation.

Mr. Rossiter, while engaged in his daily duties as schoolmaster, also encouraged the people to apply themselves to the cultivation of the land, and to raise field and garden products for the yearly show which he instituted. Both by advice and example he won encouraging success. Under his skillful hand the wild confusion of the neglected government garden gave place to order and beauty, and the rich, ripe clusters of luscious grapes bore witness to the careful attention that was bestowed on them.

James Dawe, the miller, did not find his business a very lucrative one. Almost the first effort was to repair the water mill and the adjoining dam, which had suffered from long neglect. The mill was soon put in working order, saving thereby a great deal of labor. But some disagreement arose between the miller and the party of men who worked with him, which resulted in his leaving the island, with his family, after a stay of less than two years. As for the stone mason, there was no employment for him on the island, so, after repairing a broken wall or two, he left again for Sydney, where he found good employment and wages.

A new enterprise was undertaken by the quondam Pitcairners. Observing that a great number of whales frequented the waters around the island at certain seasons of the year, they decided to purchase boats and every necessary article needed for the capture of these monsters. They showed ready skill in this new undertaking, and succeeded well from the first. The oil obtained a ready market both in Sydney and in Auckland.

HO! FOR PITCAIRN

CHAPTER XIII.

IN the meanwhile two families had returned to their old home. The superior advantages enjoyed in their new home, the greater household conveniences, the larger educational privileges, the easier access to and communication with the outside world, all failed to weigh as much with them as the wish to see once more the place that they loved as *home*. The families consisted of Moses Young, his wife and five young children, and Mayhew Young, who had married the widow of Matthew McCoy, their infant daughter, and six other children by the woman's first husband. These made up the first return party, sixteen souls in all, four males and twelve females. Three daughters of the former Mrs. McCoy remained on Norfolk Island, the two elder ones with their husbands, and the youngest to be married. Had the children been consulted in the matter, every one old enough to think would have chosen to remain, but the only alternative was to obey and follow their parents.

A much larger party had at first decided to return, and had already conveyed their goods on board the vessel that was to bear them away, but the tears and persuasions of the friends from whom they were about to part were more than they were able to resist, so they did not leave, as they had at first intended. The parting was sad. One last gathering in the church where they had worshiped for two years, one last mingling of their voices together in the parting song, which was falteringly sung, while sobs choked the utterance and tears dimmed the sight, and then the final prayer was uttered in tremulous tones and with tender earnestness by the lips of their faithful pastor, Mr. Nobbs, commending the departing company to God's care. Thus was the first separation effected between the people that for sixty years had been dwelling together like one family, sharing each other's joys and sorrows— the first separation, that held out no hope of ever meeting again. The schooner *Mary Ann*, which took them away, left on the second day of December, 1858, and reached her destination on the seventeenth day of the following month, January, 1859, making a passage of forty-six days.

The few men that first landed from the schooner had been but a short time on shore when they saw a boat, well manned, approaching the landing place at Bounty Bay. The boat's crew, as they soon discovered, belonged to a French vessel, the *Josephine*.

FAMILY GROUP OF NATIVES.

Closely following the first boat came another, but, meeting with some accident at the landing place, the boats soon returned to their ship, and she sailed away, much to the relief and satisfaction of the two families who had come to stay, and who were not a little dismayed at the thought of the stranger being so near to them.

The two families and their belongings were soon safely landed. An inspection of the deserted village showed unmistakable proofs that the island had been inhabited by someone for a short time, at least, subsequent to the removal of the former inhabitants. A keg of salt, some old crockery gathered from the deserted houses, and sundry other household articles had been brought together, evidently for the use of someone in need. Some of the houses had been destroyed by fire, while others had been broken down. These were all so many evidences that the island had been lately occupied The matter, however, was soon cleared up. A slate was picked up in the schoolroom whereon was written with some iron instrument the names of some men who had found an asylum on the island, after having lost their ship on Oeno, a low-lying coral island, surrounded by reefs, some eighty miles northwest of Pitcairn Island.

Further particulars were afterwards obtained, first, from an American sailor who was left on the island by the captain of the whale ship *Hiawatha*, and later from a copy of the *Friend*, sent to the island by the people's faithful friend, the Rev. Samuel C. Damon, of

Honolulu, Hawaiian Islands.   In the *Friend* was the
account of the loss of the *Wildwave* on Oeno Island.
The ship was under command of Captain J N. Knowles,
who, in the early part of 1858, was on a voyage from
San Francisco to one of the Eastern States, and who,
having lost his ship, came with such of the crew as were
willing to Pitcairn Island, where they stayed until a
boat had been constructed of such materials as the
island afforded, to convey them to Tahiti, whence a
passage home could be found.

About twenty-three years afterwards one of the
lads who had returned with the first party, now grown
into a middle-aged man, was in San Francisco.   While
there he called at the office of Captain Knowles, and
heard from that gentleman's own lips the following
interesting account of their enforced detention on Pitcairn Island:—

The *Wildwave* was outward bound from San Francisco, when she became a wreck on the reefs of Oeno
Island.   Besides the captain, officers, and crew, there
were ten passengers, numbering in all about thirty-
seven persons, all of whom landed safely on the island.
The remains of a brother of Captain Knowles, which
were being carried home for interment, were also taken
on shore and buried.   The headstone that accompanied the body was also set to mark the last resting
place of the dead.   When everything that could contribute to their comfort had been landed, the shipwrecked men proceeded at once to make the best of
the circumstances.   Abundant food supplies had been

brought ashore from the ship, and if that should fail before help could come, the large numbers of birds, as well as of fish, were sufficient to keep them from starvation.

But the captain felt that some immediate action must be taken, and so, as speedily as possible, a boat was made ready and provisioned, and himself, Mr. Bartlett, the first mate, the carpenter, and four seamen bade good-by to the thirty men left on Oeno, and came on to Pitcairn Island, to obtain if possible help for themselves and their companions. The captain, by a wise forethought, had, before leaving, taken the second mate and others to mark the spot where three or four birds were sitting on their eggs. These birds were then secured and taken along with the party in the boat, to be their news carriers in the event of their reaching their destined place in safety. This they did. They landed on the west side of the island, and the boat was drawn up only a few yards from the water's edge, as it was the captain's intention to return as soon as possible to Oeno. This plan, however, was frustrated by an unlooked-for calamity.

The captain's and mate's first care after dragging the boat to the place where it was to be left, was to take out from it all their nautical instruments, and then, taking the birds in their hands, they started on their way up the high hill leading to the village. Strips of leather had been prepared on which to send the message of their safe arrival to their companions on Oeno. These missives having been securely fas-

10

tened to the birds, they were let go, and the party
stood somewhat anxiously watching them take their
flight.   At first the unusual encumbrance seemed
likely to impede their progress, and the watchers saw
them "turn round and round as if stunned a little," but
they soon regained their wonted manner, and the men
had the satisfaction of seeing the birds take their way
in the direct line whence they had come.   In time the
men on Oeno had the pleasure of learning of the safety
of the little band who had gone to Pitcairn, but the
hope of soon seeing them again was not realized, and
many months of weary watching passed ere further
word reached them.

Meanwhile, the seven men, after seeing to the safe
flight of the birds, proceeded on their way.   Arriving
at the top of the hill, they looked down on the little
village of thatched cottages nestling among orange
trees.   These trees, even at that distance, were seen
to be loaded with golden fruit.   The sight was a very
pleasant one to the shipwrecked men, but no rising
smoke gave evidence that the place was inhabited.   A
few minutes' quick walking brought them down to
the silent houses, where not a human being was seen.
For a day or two they remained in the deserted village,
intending soon to return to their companions on Oeno;
but the mate, having occasion to go over to the west
side, found to his dismay that the boat, which had
been left too near the water, had been not only reached
by the heavy surf that had arisen in their absence,
but was broken beyond repair.

This unlooked-for disaster was the cause of grave anxiety, and all that could be done was to go to work and construct another boat. This was a very difficult matter, as materials and tools were scant and poor. To obtain nails some of the houses were broken down, and others were burned. Trees were cut down, and as the men had no saws, the ax was made to do duty for both saw and ax, thus occasioning great loss of time and material. But in spite of the many drawbacks, the work went steadily and bravely on.

At length the boat was finished. The sail of the broken boat, and such odds and ends as could be found in the houses, made up the rigging of the little craft, which was named the *John Adams*. The trappings of the old pulpit in the church supplied the red, and a bit of blue calico taken from off an old bedstead served for the ground, on which were arranged the white stars of the American flag; and so, with the stars and stripes to float from the mast of their small vessel, it was launched, after months of weary, anxious work and waiting, rendered doubly anxious by the knowledge that the loved ones at home were pining in suspense and uncertainty regarding their fate.

Two of the men, afraid of venturing in the boat they had helped to build, stayed behind until help from a more reliable source could come to them. Owing to adverse winds, Captain Knowles did not return to Oeno, as he had at first intended, but steered for Tahiti instead, making a brief call at the island of Nukahiva on the way. At Tahiti they found the

U. S. sloop of war *Vandalia*. The story of the shipwreck and subsequent facts was soon told, and the
Vandalia went at once to the rescue. Mr. Bartlett,
the mate of the *Wildwave*, also went with the rescuing
party, who in due time reached Oeno, where they
found all the thirty men alive and well. These having
been received on board, the *Vandalia* went to Pitcairn
Island, where the other two men of the crew were,
both of whom were enjoying excellent health, but
glad to leave the place that was so lonely and isolated.

After Captain Knowles had reached Tahiti, he did
not delay to take the first opportunity to go home, as
he was extremely anxious about his wife, an anxiety
which was only too well founded, for the poor lady had
died of hopeless grief and suspense concerning the
fate of her husband.

AN UNPLEASANT SURPRISE

CHAPTER XIV.

N the course of our narrative
we now return to the two
families on Pitcairn. Their
first night on shore was passed in one of the old
houses which was so thickly covered with a growth
of the wild bean that all felt sure it would afford the
best protection against rain, if rain should fall. But
they were soon convinced of their mistake when, during the night, a pouring rain roused them from their
slumbers by coming in upon them through the frail
covering of the vines. Early the next day they
removed to another house, which afforded better
accommodations, and where they stayed until their
own cottages were repaired. They had but just finished the work of arranging their new abode to the
best advantage when some of the young girls sallied
forth, accompanied by one of their mothers, to have a
look around the forsaken place When only a short

(145)

distance from the house, they espied, coming towards them through the bush-grown path, two men, who had just come ashore from a ship, unknown to any of the party on the island. At sight of the strangers, one of whom was carrying a gun, the other being a colored man, the woman and girls screamed and fled, one of the girls in her terror dropping several feet from the boughs of an orange tree up which she had climbed.

Impelled by a haunting dread that something awful was about to happen, they ran in breathless haste toward the house where the other woman and children were. Their frightened looks told plainly enough that something unusual had occurred, and, crowded close together, the story of what they had seen was repeated. But they congratulated themselves on the fact that their retreat would not be easily discovered, as the path was well nigh hidden from view by the thick growth of weeds and bushes. Worst of all, their natural protectors were all absent from home at the time. Their terror could be better imagined than described when, a few minutes having passed, the black man's face appeared through an opening in the trees, and immediately behind him was his white companion. The lot of timid women and children could scarce refrain from shrieking aloud, but the colored man assured them, with a pleasant smile, that there was nothing to fear, and that the gun was brought on shore for other game than themselves. It did not take long to quiet their fears, when they discovered that the black man was really a pleasant-spoken, kindly person; but the other man held aloof, and scarcely had a word to say.   They both gladly accepted food from the hands of the women, who also gave them permission to take all the fruit that they wished.

The visitors informed them that they had just come ashore from a whaler, the *William Wirt*, and had brought their ammunition with them for the purpose of obtaining game.   Another whale ship came in on the same day, and their respective crews carried back to their ships a large supply of animal food, which they had taken in hunting, viz., goats, fowls, and fish, as all were so easily obtained on account of their great numbers.

The search for hens' eggs gave much pleasant occupation to the young people, as the island was nearly overrun by the immense increase of fowls; nor were the older folk less active in going out on an egg hunt than the children.   Life for them seemed one continuous round of present enjoyment.   There was scarcely any need for work, as the island produced in lavish abundance more than sufficient, both of animal and vegetable food, for their every want—goats, sheep, fowls, and plenty of fish, which had become tame through having been left so long in their undisturbed freedom.   One obstacle in the way of the young people's pleasures was the presence of the few cattle on the island, the mere sight of which was enough to make them run for refuge to the nearest tree, if not within easy distance of their homes. As the island is too small to allow the increase of cattle upon it, it was thought best to extirpate them; and, most unwisely, the doomed cattle were in time all destroyed.

During those years the productiveness of the island

BREADFRUIT.

was remarkable. The breadfruit, yams, potatoes, taro, as well as the delicious fruits that grew on the island, seemed untouched by the curse. It did not seem possible that in a few years a change so complete could take place as to affect almost the entire productions of the island. But so it was. Being abundantly provided with food supplies, with scarcely an effort of their own, the two families had not much to do. The making of

tappa, however, gave employment to all during three
or four months of the year, and heavy work it was too,
with all the various processes through which it passed.
A description of the work may be given here.

First, the plants must be cut down and divested of
their bark. Each bark is then peeled and the inner
portion beaten out until it becomes soft, and the fibers
separate. Washing is the next thing, and this is
repeated until every trace of the abundant sap is
removed. By this time the substance has widened to
five times its natural width, and has a beautiful lace-
like appearance. It is then wrapped up in the large
leaves of the *appi* (*arum gigantum*), sufficient being
inclosed in the wrap to make a sheet. Being allowed
to remain for a few days, it becomes soft and almost
pulpy. Then it is ready to lay out in strips of the
required length, one bark being laid over another
until the proper thickness is obtained. The whole is
then beaten out, two persons being required to do this,
as they stand on the opposite sides of a large, long,
and smoothly planed log, called a "dood-a," and with
their heavy beaters keeping time with the utmost
exactness. The work is noisy and tiresome. When
each sheet is finished, it is hardened by spreading out
daily in the sun. This is continued until the paper-
like fabric can bear washing. To render it tough it
is dyed, the dye being obtained by steeping the red
inner bark of the *doodooee* (candlenut tree) in water.
When dry the dye has a reddish brown color, which is
very pretty when fresh.

Most of this disagreeable work was performed by the two mothers of the families, as they could not trust the delicate work of handling the easily injured sheets to the inexperienced hands of the young girls. These, from the age of eight to thirteen, grew up in almost entire ignorance of the art of sewing, and this for the good reason that they had nothing to learn with. Thread was too precious to waste in teaching the children to sew, and should the few needles break or be lost, there was no prospect of replacing them; besides, every bit of calico which might be used for the purpose of learning to sew was carefully hoarded as a future patch for the garment, which only too readily became threadbare. Usually a slit in the sleeve or side of a frock or petticoat was drawn together by means of a string which the fibrous bark of the *boo-ron* tree supplied. But these girls enjoyed their wild, free life notwithstanding, and were happy in the possession of perfect health, plenty to eat and drink, and their garments, if poor, and even ragged, were kept as clean as the nature of their duties allowed, while in their persons they were particularly clean.

Living such a free, wild life as they did, and with so much idle time on their hands, it is not to be wondered at that the young people, unaided, would turn their attention to books, and seek to educate their minds in the knowledge to be gained from them. This fact caused much anxiety to two, at least, of their number, Sarah McCoy, the oldest girl, and also her brother.

These two young people had been members of Mrs
Selwyn's class during their two years' stay on Norfolk
Island, and nothing had caused them more regret on
leaving that place than the fact that they were by
their removal cut off from so many of the educational
advantages obtained there, having just experienced
enough of the pleasures of knowledge to make them
long for more. Urged by the necessities of the case
to do what they could, these two young persons collected what books they thought would help them,
which they found in the old schoolroom, together with
slates and pencils, and opened a school in Mr. Nobbs'
former study, for a class of six or seven girls and one
boy, giving them lessons in reading, writing, and spelling, teaching them also addition, subtraction, multipli-
cation, and division.

But searching for hens' eggs, taking care of chickens, running with a wheelbarrow down some steep
hill, swinging on the long hanging roots of the great
banyan trees, and other employments of a like nature, were far more congenial to the tastes of the
lively, healthy, and active-limbed children than to
sit droning lazily over their books and drawling out
"Ab-ba, father," and so on; and when for some mis-
behavior the youthful teacher would remonstrate, he
would be greeted with a derisive laugh; or should he
attempt to administer the rod, he would be met with
such a spirit of defiance that his attempts at punishment would be useless. Such scenes usually ended in
the unruly scholar climbing with the agility of a cat

up the posts of the house, where he would look down upon his teacher and feel secure from the well-merited punishment.

CHILDREN AND WHEELBARROW.

In spite of such untoward behavior from the older children, the long-suffering teachers succeeded in accomplishing what they had set themselves to do, and had the satisfaction of seeing their trying pupils accomplish the task of learning to write, in addition to their being able to read. They also learned to spell fairly well, and were able to master the simpler rules in arithmetic. In October, 1860, H. M. S. *Calypso* visited the island, staying a few hours. The chaplain

of the ship came on shore, and manifested much interest in regard to the religious instruction of the children and their right bringing up. On leaving, the kind
visitors supplied the little school with books, slates
and pencils, copy books, pens, penholders, and ink, a
gift which was thoroughly appreciated and most
thankfully received.

On Sundays the two families met for worship in
Moses Young's house, each of the two men at times
taking part in conducting the services, but more frequently the master of the house officiated, and in strict
accordance with the Church of England liturgy in
the Book of Common Prayer.

Moses Young, who owned a fife, on which he often
discoursed sweet music, was also an excellent performer
on the fiddle. To the ability he possessed of playing
with considerable skill on these his favorite instruments,
was added a limited knowledge of written music,
gained under the able leadership of Mr. Hugh Carleton. This knowledge he tried to put to the best
account, and formed a class, composed of the four
adults, including himself, and as many of the young
people as wished to come, to whom he taught the
gamut. Having drilled his little class in "do, re, mi,
fa, sol, la, si, do," and learning the skips, *ad infinitum*,
he made a sudden advance to a few of the old standard church tunes, and succeeded in reviving, for the
benefit of his youthful learners, the old tunes of Truro
and Clarendon, and teaching them an entirely new
tune besides. He did not accomplish more of his

laudable undertaking, probably because his pupils did
not give him the needed encouragement, or else he
himself checked their ardor, as he did in the following instance.   One night at the close of the usual
drill, and before the class was dismissed, the teacher
proposed that they should sing the National Anthem.
Sundry efforts were made before the proper pitch was
obtained.   At last the tune was fairly started, and the
anthem sung.   The closing lines,—

> "Shed o'er her heart a ray
> Of wisdom's glorious day;
> Loved be Victoria's sway—
> God save the Queen,"

were sung in a manner expressive of the singers' entire
satisfaction in the performance.   Their leader, however, thought differently, and, waiting until the last
notes had ceased, he turned to his pupils a face beam-
ing with hardly-suppressed mirth, and remarked,
"Your singing sounds just like the noise made by a
swarm of big flies."   He then burst into a merry peal
of laughter, in which he was joined by his whole class.

In October, 1862, H. M. S. *Charybdis* paid a short
visit to the island.   It being impossible to land at
Bounty Bay, the visitors went around to the west side,
where the first half of the way led up a steep, high
hill.   But the walk was cheerfully accomplished, and
a warm hospitality was extended them when they
reached the little village, a substantial repast of the best
that the island afforded being prepared for them.   The
two humble homes were made to look their best, and

the carefully hoarded linen and cotton sheets were brought out and displayed upon the beds, in honor of the visitors.

The *Charybdis* stayed only a day, taking a good supply of all that the island produced. So fruitful was the little island at the time of their visit that the officers declared that it seemed "like a little Garden of Eden." A printed account of the visit of the *Charybdis* to Pitcairn was sent to Norfolk Island. The news, when received, after the long silence of nearly five years, created an excitement among relatives and friends not to be described, and smiles and tears followed each other in quick succession as the short but interesting description of the old home and the loved ones there was read and reread to ears and hearts that seemed never to grow weary of listening.

THE SECOND PARTY RETURNS

CHAPTER XV.

TIME passed on, and again preparations were being made at Norfolk
for the second return party to Pitcairn Island. Four families decided
to go. These were, first, Thursday O. Christian, his
wife and nine children. Mrs. Christian's aged mother
also accompanied them for the purpose of seeing
again her son, Mayhew Young, who was of the first
party. The old lady was Elizabeth Mills, only
daughter of John Mills, of the *Bounty*, and the son
whom she was going to see was one named in affectionate remembrance of her much esteemed and well-
remembered friend, Captain Mayhew Folger, who had
discovered the colony on Pitcairn Island fifty-five
years before. The other families were Robert Buffett
and his wife, Samuel Warren and his wife, who was
the daughter of T. O. Christian. These last mentioned
persons were married to each other on the eve of leaving Norfolk Island. In addition to those above men-

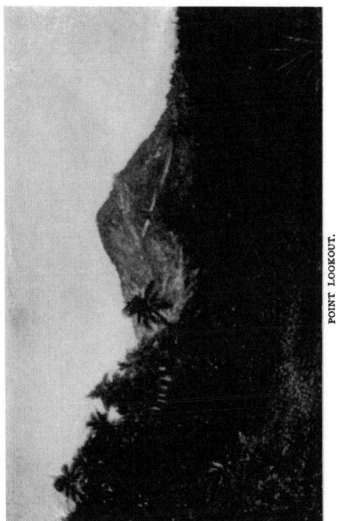

POINT LOOKOUT.

tioned were Simon Young, his mother (Hannah Adams), his wife, and eight children.   The number of persons composing the second party was twenty-seven.   Their friends were strongly opposed to their leaving, and did all in their power to induce them to stay.

The last mentioned family was amongst the first that had decided upon returning, and had taken the first steps in preparing to return; but the fact that the passage fare by the first vessel was not paid out of his own money had enough weight with Simon Young to decide his waiting until he was able to defray the expense of the passage for both himself and family.

Having had some little experience in teaching children in the week-day school, besides being for years a Sunday school teacher, he was greatly concerned also about the welfare of the young people that had preceded him to the old home, and the thought of their need, as well as his own deep-seated love of *home*, seemed to urge him to take the present step.   In vain did relatives and friends place before the parents the question of the future welfare of their children; their decision was made, the passage already engaged, and the thought of again withdrawing was not to be allowed.

Nor were their relatives alone opposed to their going.   In a letter sent to the wife of Simon Young Mrs. Selwyn expressed, not her opinion only, but the opinions of both Bishop Selwyn and Bishop Patteson as well, in regard to the ministration of the word of

God, and the ordinances attending thereon.   Speaking
of the "important news" that reached them in New
Zealand, she says: "I will not conceal that it has made
me very, very sorry.   I never, like all the rest of us,
had but one opinion about the return to Pitcairn's
Island, and you know full well what that opinion is;
and I am more concerned than I can say to find that
your family are to be foremost in the next departure.
To both the bishops and to myself does it seem a very
serious responsibility for anyone voluntarily to put
himself and his family out of the reach of all the means
of grace appointed by our Lord himself as necessary
to us.   It is a very different matter if he find himself
bereft of them through no fault or design of his own,
as you all were in the old days of Pitcairn."

Writing on the same subject, Bishop Patteson thus
expresses himself in a letter to Simon Young: "I fear
that you do not feel the real importance of this point
on which I so greatly insist," *i. e.,* "*the most essential
thing of all—the authorized ministration of the word
and sacraments.*"   "You may or may not think that
the ministrations of Bishop Selwyn, or me, or Mr.
Nobbs, are edifying—that is not to the point.   It is
Christ himself, who by the hands of His ministers,
regularly appointed, gives to His own people His own
blessings.   If you willfully, and by your own act,
deprive yourself and family of this blessing, how shall
you receive the blessing?   Christ gives it in His own
appointed way; what right have you or anyone to neg·
lect His way, and yet think to receive the blessing?

"And if you are not doing right in going away from such privileges, you may be sure that you will not be doing good to others. You will be encouraging them in a course that is not right. You ought to be using whatever influence you have to keep others from going from the blessings which you have at Norfolk Island, and will *not* have at Pitcairn Island.

"And with reference to what you say about the 'path marked out by God.' My dear friend, oftentimes a man makes up his mind really on some point, though he is hardly willing to allow to himself that he has done so; and then, with a design already settled in his mind—seeks for advice and direction. . . . Now if you have any doubt about the course you propose to follow, and you *must* have doubts, you *must* see that it cannot be right to leave the blessings I have spoken of—you cannot make what is wrong appear right by any other process than one of self-deception.

"Your object is to do those who have gone some good. But if God's blessing go not with you, you cannot and will not do them good; and if it be wrong to go, it is wrong to encourage others to go. Why are you 'sorry that they went'? Not only because they have left their friends, but you are, I hope, sorry because they are living on apart from the regular ministrations of the church. But you cannot supply that want; you add only to the number of those who are in want. You disapprove their conduct, and yet follow it. But you think you go to help them. No, my friend, by doing what is at least doubtful, if not wrong, you are very far from helping them. You injure yourself and your family, and you encourage those that are gone to think lightly of the error they have committed.

GROUP OF YOUNG MEN.

"I have written strongly, but you know why. If I have said the truth, may God bless it to the good of us both."

This letter, written in such plain and strong language, and which showed such solicitude for the spiritual welfare of those who were on the eve of leaving, did not fail to make a deep impression, yet not so as to convince that the step about to be taken was a wrong one.

As for their own pastor, Mr. Nobbs, he had strongly opposed the return of the first two families, but now was rather willing than otherwise that the rest should follow. Indeed, far from discouraging such a step, he was glad that someone could be found who would voluntarily go and, to the best of his ability, instruct the children who were growing up so far from educational privileges. Quickly the day drew on that was to witness another painful separation. As in the first case, the young people of the second return party did not share the feelings of their parents. Pitcairn Island possessed no attraction for them, and Norfolk Island, which was *home* to them, was rendered doubly dear because of the many loved companions and friends that were to be left behind.

One sore trial to Simon Young and his wife and family was the separation from the eldest son, a youth of eighteen years of age, who, with a son of Mr. Nobbs, was left with Bishop Patteson, to be by him trained and fitted for a life of future usefulness in the work of the mission. It was the young man's own choice and resolve to remain with the bishop, who, both to his companion and himself, had ever showed the kind and tender consideration of a parent in everything regarding their best interests. So, however sad the parting or sharp the trial, the parents knew that their son was in good hands, and Bishop Patteson had written that, as far as they could supply it, both himself and Mrs.

Selwyn would fill the place of parents to him. His
companion had always been to him as a dear brother.*

And now the time had come for the final parting.
Once more grief-stricken friends assembled in the
church, which would know the presence of some of
them no more forever, to implore the divine aid and
blessing upon all, but more especially to commend the
departing friends to the care and keeping of their faithful God. The hymn, composed by Mr. Nobbs and
sung on the former occasion, was again sung, the two
last stanzas of which are given here, these referring
directly to those about to leave, being composed for
this special farewell gathering :—

---

*Edwin Nobbs and Fisher Young joined the Melanesian Mission under its
first bishop, the Right Rev. J. C Patteson, the former to become, probably,
the successor of his father, the Rev. G. H. Nobbs, pastor of the church on Norfolk Island. But it was not to be   In less than four years after joining the
mission, the bishop paid a visit to the island of Santa Cruz, and found the
natives hostile to their landing. On the bishop's first visit the natives had
shown themselves friendly, but now, August, 1864, a sudden and unexpected
attack was made by the natives against their visitors, and the young men.
Edwin and Fisher, were wounded, the former in his left cheek, the latter in
his left wrist. An Englishman, Pierce by name, was wounded in the chest,
but he recovered. Fisher died on the eighth day, after suffering the dreadful
agonies of lockjaw. His body was taken ashore at Port Patteson and buried
there. His deeply-sorrowing companion attended the funeral, the exposure
bringing on a cold which resulted in the same dire disease. Everything that
the most loving care could suggest was done for them, but in vain   The
bishop, writing of that sad time, said, "Never have I known such sorrow,
never have I been so broken down with overmuch sorrow." They both died
in the arms of the bishop, almost the last words of each being a prayer for
their murderers. Edwin was buried at sea. It can truly be said of them that

> " Lovely and pleasant they were in their lives,
>   And in death they were not divided."

The deservedly-loved Bishop Patteson himself fell a victim to the murderous
assault of the natives, on the 20th of September, 1871, seven years after the
death of the young men.

"For those who in the flesh remain,
    Though absent from our sight,
For their remembrance we'll retain
    Affections pure and bright;
Though parted, severed, far away,
    Perchance to meet no more,
For their prosperity we'll pray,
    And love them as before.

"Again dissevered is the tie;
    Brethren and sisters part;
The mournful separation nigh
    Pervades with grief each heart;
Here, now, beneath this sacred roof
    Fresh blessings we implore,
Beneath our tears the fervent proof,
    'We'll love you as before.'"

In the large company that had gathered for the last farewell service, there was scarcely an eye that was not dim with tears. Brothers and sisters, as well as parents and children, who had never known what separation meant were now about to experience its pain. Perhaps no one felt the bitterness of parting more than did the two aged mothers, Elizabeth Young and Hannah Young, who were leaving behind them children that were most dear, to return to the far-distant home of their childhood. The night after the farewell meeting was a wakeful one for those whom the parting most nearly concerned, as the morrow would witness the departure. The morning dawned only too soon. The whole community, including all the other families that had recently settled among them, accompanied the party that was leaving, down to the pier. Loud sobs and many tears told what a heavy trial the separation was. At last all was over—the last fond embrace, the lingering kiss, the warm hand clasp—and the voyagers embarked in their small vessel to return to the isolated island whither the two other families had preceded them six years before. Two men, relatives of the families who were leaving, came with them on a visit.

One death took place before the voyage was ended, that of a child of Thursday Christian, that had been ailing for some time before leaving Norfolk Island. At the mother's request, the captain kindly consented to preserve the body, to be brought and laid with others of her children in the graveyard at Pitcairn Island. The body was put in a barrel, and this was placed in the forepart of the ship on deck, and was for some time an object of terror to the superstitious minds of the young people on board, who wondered how the mother dared to approach the spot in the dead of night and weep over her child there. By degrees, however, the feelings of awe and fear wore away, and as the little ship neared the end of her voyage, there remained but the wish that the gentle child had been spared to reach the place whither they were going. And, too, the sorrow of parting from friends on Norfolk Island gradually lost its bitterness as the thought of soon seeing again their long-separated friends was cherished. Still the frequent sigh and the silent tear told that the dear ones were not forgotten. Especially touching was it to see the two old ladies, who had no growing families to engross their thoughts, sit together and weep silent tears, as the aged will, over the sons and daughters they were to see no more.

The Reception

CHAPTER XVI.

THE schooner *St. Kilda,* which conveyed the second return party to Pitcairn Island, leaving Norfolk Island on the 18th of December, 1863, reached its destination on the 2d of February, 1864, the voyage being on the whole a pleasant one. It was night when the little ship reached the end of her voyage, a beautiful night, calm and clear, and the unsuspecting folks on shore did not dream of seeing on the morrow the long absent faces of relatives and friends, and were preparing to retire to rest when a musket's sharp report from over the water broke the stillness. On board all was excitement and bustle, muskets firing, the young men hallooing and burning flash lights to attract the attention of those on shore, even calling some of them by their names, as the vessel was close to the land.

The perfect Babel of sounds soon succeeded in rousing, not the peaceful inhabitants only, but their terror as well. Leaving their homes, they hurried down to that part of the land overlooking the sea, whence the noise proceeded, to try to find out the cause of such a commotion. An undefinable dread took possession of their hearts when they saw the lights and heard the repeated sharp reports of the muskets across the water. The children were cautioned not to expose themselves, but to remain hidden behind the thick shrubs and trees, lest a stray ball should hit them, for they did not know that nothing but powder was put in the barrels. No answering response was made from the shore to those on board, the frightened islanders deeming it more prudent to maintain perfect silence and wait until morning to learn the cause of all the disturbance.

Very early the next morning two of the men went off in their canoes, and were agreeably surprised to find that the formidable foe of the previous night was only a party of old friends come to settle again in their former home. As soon as possible the boat was lowered and the passengers taken ashore. They were not a little amused to find that the girls on the island had by no means recovered from their fright, but, on the approach of the first persons who landed, ran away in different directions to hide themselves, and could scarcely be persuaded by their mothers to come out and greet their friends. By degrees, however, their extreme shyness wore off, and soon they were chatting away with one another about all that had taken place since their long separation.

With the exception that the once-cultivated grounds

were all overrun with weeds, and the houses mostly were in ruins, there did not seem to be, to the eyes of the older people, at least, any change in the island. But to the younger people the change from the island they had just left made a great impression, the dwelling houses and kitchens, in their ugly bareness and smoke-begrimed appearance, contrasting unfavorably with the neatly-built houses and tidy kitchens they had been accustomed to. The ovens, too, where most of the cooking was done were only holes dug in the ground, the required heat being obtained from a number of small stones which were placed over a pile of wood after the fire had been kindled to heat the stones. The covering for such ovens consists of leaves, and over these a thick layer of earth, which effectually prevents the escape of the steam, which so thoroughly and so well cooks the food that is placed within.

The appearance, too, of the little village was so different from the place where they had lately lived! Instead of a long row of houses neatly standing side by side, facing a broad and well-paved street, here were only a few humbly-thatched dwellings—only two of which were habitable—half hidden amongst the thick growth of trees which surrounded them. But the general appearance, so different, was none the less beautiful, and the sight of the orange groves, displaying their wealth of golden fruit, was a very pleasing picture to the young folks, who had never seen such a sight before. Near to these could be seen the breadfruit

trees, with their large, beautiful leaves, growing side
by side with the glossy, dark-leaved *fei*, or mountain
plantain, its heavy bunch of fruit being supported in
an upright position by a stout stalk shooting direct
from the center of the leaves, while here and there a
cocoanut tree lent its graceful aid to beautify the
scenery.   Towering over all, and lovely in their delicate, light-green foliage, were the wide-spreading
branches of the mighty banyan tree, whose roots, as
they hang from the boughs overhead, prove such a
strong temptation to the boys and girls to go swinging on them.   Sometimes an accident happens when
swinging on the roots of the banyan trees, but in no
instance has it ended fatally, and in one case only
were there any bones broken.

Everything about the island, and the manner of
cooking and living in general, interested the young
people greatly.   Never before had they heard such a
chorus of cock crowing in the early morning, or the
endless chirpings of numberless chickens, as they followed their busy, clucking mothers.   The boys and
girls, to whom such a free, wild life was a desirable
change from the confinement of a long voyage, entered
heartily into the fun of going out in search of hens'
eggs, an abundance of which was found all over the
island.   The time to them passed quickly, like one
long holiday, for in the unsettled state of things they
were not confined to any school duties.

There was much to hear and tell on both sides.
One story that greatly interested the newcomers was

that of a Peruvian ship, loaded with natives, that came
to Pitcairn from Easter Island the year before, 1863.
The captain of the ship, on coming near enough,
ordered a boat to be lowered and manned. He himself went in the boat to seek for a landing place. The
people on shore observing the boat approaching, two
men went off in a canoe to meet the strangers. The
captain accosted them with the question, "Can you
speak *Anglice?*" Receiving an answer in the affirma-
tive, he said that he was going ashore to see if he
could get some sugar cane for a load of slaves he had
on board, whom, he informed them, he was taking to
their homes. On coming ashore he tried by many
arguments to persuade every member of the two families to accompany him back to the ship, where,
he assured them, they would receive kind treatment.
One thing he objected to was their knowledge of the
English language, and he told them also that their
skins were not as dark as he expected to find them.

The captain's entreaties for them to go on board, and
his oft-repeated expressions of kindness toward them,
served to arouse their suspicions, and they firmly
declined; however, the two men who had been to
meet the boat went on board the ship. There they
saw a sight which they could not easily forget.
Numbers of poor natives of different ages, from quite
young children to men and women in and beyond
middle life, many of whom were entirely naked,
were crowded into the close and stifling hold of the
ship. Those who were not entirely naked had a

waistcloth only for their covering. All seemed sad,
and their countenances bore the trace of much sorrow,
and had a look of hopeless misery. The atmosphere
of the place where the poor natives were confined was
very unwholesome from want of fresh air, and many
of the slaves were suffering from a distressing cough
that shook their frames. The captain told them that
he was going to the Gambier Islands, on his way to
restore the poor creatures to their homes.

It was not until many years had passed that the
truth about the ship and her business was made
known. The natives were being taken to the Peruvian Coast to work as slaves, and the captain was trying to get all he could to go with him. Long afterwards some of the survivors returned to their home
on Easter Island, but with their return were introduced certain diseases which until then had been
unknown among their people. So their home coming
was as much a cause of regret as of rejoicing.

While the two families on Pitcairn Island were
blessed with robust health and plenty of food, their
clothing was very scanty, and was made to do service
long after it was threadbare, and while scarcely of sufficient body to hold together. Their very limited supply
was obtained from whale ships that once in a long while
would call in to obtain fresh provisions. On one
occasion they were imposed upon in the following
manner: The captain of a certain whale ship, requiring
something fresh in the way of fruit and other things,
called in at the island to obtain a supply. He took

from the islanders one hundred and eighteen fowls, a number of hogs, about eighteen barrels in all of yams and potatoes, and large quantities of fruit, the getting of which and carrying them down to the landing place occupied the handful of men and women and the few children that were old enough to help, for a whole week. The people were sorely in need of clothing, which could very well have been sold them in payment of what they gave, but they received in return about sixteen yards of calico, three boxes of soap, two of which carried together just made a comfortable load for a boy to carry, and the bargain was finished by the addition of a coil of rope and two half worn-out tubs, which served the purpose of emptying the mud out from the wells on the island that required cleaning. The captain pleaded hard times as an excuse for what he gave, and the people had to be satisfied with such an explanation. But in telling the story afterwards many a hearty laugh was had at their own expense, seeing how easily they were imposed upon and how they took it as a matter of course.

AT HOME AGAIN

VISIT OF H.M.S. SUTLEJ

CHAPTER XVII.

AS was to be expected, the first weeks that followed the arrival of the second party were very busy weeks indeed. They were housed as well as could be managed in the two small dwellings of the families that first came. But the inconveniences attendant on such crowded accommodations were cheerfully borne. In a short time a temporary abode for each family of the newcomers had been erected, into which they removed until their permanent homes should have been built. As all the men and boys took hold of the work, willingly and cheerfully helping each other, the building business progressed rapidly.

A pleasant break in the busy weeks was the visit of Admiral Sir John Kingcome in his flagship, the *Sutlej*, on the 29th of March, 1864. The day was perfect, with scarce a ripple on the sea, and the sky was wearing its loveliest blue. The sight of the large boats crowded with men going and returning between the shore and the ship, was greatly enjoyed by the islanders. A large crowd both of officers and men landed, and all seemed to enjoy their visit much, and they gladly availed themselves of the privilege of taking free whatever the island produced. The young gentlemen manifested a great deal of interest in the preparation of a dinner gotten up for them in the island style, especially that part of it which consisted of the dressing of a pig and cooking it in the primitive underground oven, a favorite mode of cooking meat among the people.

In the afternoon, as the people had been kindly invited to visit the ship, nearly all went on board, and had a delightful time visiting the different parts of the large vessel, and listening with thrilling pleasure to the band as it discoursed sweetest music The visit of the *Sutlej* was opportune as regarded one young man, at least. He had a wound in the right knee which threatened to prove fatal, but the surgeon of the ship, having examined it, probed the wound and applied the proper remedies. The cure that followed was rapid and complete. In the long interval that followed the admiral's coming, when the islanders seemed to have been shut completely out from the rest of the world, the pleasure that his visit gave still remained as a bright spot in the round of their monotonous lives.

At this time the chief concern of the people was to build a suitable house for public worship. Services were held in one of the dwelling houses, which, although there was room enough to accommodate comfortably the two families that had first come, was now too small for the increased number of worshipers. As soon, then, as these later arrivals had been settled with some degree of comfort, the work of building the church and schoolhouse combined began. Willing hands made light work, and, notwithstanding the lack of workers, the plain wooden structure, with thatched roof, was duly finished and consecrated to divine serv·ice. It was a glad day when the small congregation met for the first time within its humble walls to worship God, nor was the worship less fervent because above them there was only a bare, thatched roof. Simon Young now stood as leader of the people, and, in addition to his services for the spiritual welfare of the people, took upon himself the task of instructing, to the best of his ability, the youth and children in the "three R's"—reading, 'riting, and 'rithmetic. Having brought from Norfolk Island a small supply of schoolbooks, he was able with their help to guide the young and ignorant minds into the pursuit of something higher than the searching for hens' eggs and their own self-pleasing.

Possessing a fair knowledge of simple music, he also, with the small means at command, taught the children to sing. After leading them through the simplest airs. he taught them, and with great success, to sing in four parts, and the fact that out of a class of fifteen ten were able to read music by sight, gave him great encouragement in that branch of his work. Beginning

SIMON YOUNG AND WIFE.

life anew, house building and cultivating the ground for the support of a large family left him scarcely any leisure for self-improvement, but what he was able to do he did faithfully. In cultivating the land, wife and children assisted, thus lightening the heavy duties of the husband and father. No work was allowed to supersede that which was the dearest aim and object of his whole life, namely, seeking to instill knowledge into the minds of the young, and helping to train them to love what is good and pure and true, and to inspire them to search for themselves the treasures of knowledge that may be obtained in the works of other men, some few volumes of which he possessed. He also organized a Sunday school, at first taking all the labor upon himself, and, as the necessity arose, appointing others to assist him.

In December of 1864 six of the young people—three of the older settlers and three of the others—were united in the bonds of matrimony, the wedding taking place on Christmas day. To the younger portion of the community, at least, the excitement of a triple wedding was a very pleasant thing to happen to break the monotony of their quiet and secluded lives.

In 1866 a man-of-war, the *Mutine*, called at the island, bringing letters from relatives and friends on Norfolk Island, the first word that had been received from them since the parting, nearly three years before. The day was a stormy one in November—so stormy that the ship was delayed only long enough to deliver the mail, one canoe with two men in it having success-

fully passed through the heavy breakers and the tossing sea to reach the ship.   The news brought was
mostly sad, for the deaths of several dear friends were
recorded, but that which more than any other affected
the people deeply was the tidings of the death
of Edwin Nobbs and Fisher Young, who had been
shot by the natives of Santa Cruz, when, with the
bishop of Melanesia, they visited that place.   Although
the two young men had been dead two years before
the tidings reached them, the loss of their firstborn
son came upon the parents of Fisher Young with all
the shock of a sudden and unexpected bereavement,
and the heartrending cries of the mother bespoke the
grief felt for her son.   He had been consecrated to
God before his birth, and his chosen path was that of
a missionary, nor was it small comfort to his parents
that his last dying message was, "Tell my father that I
died in the path of duty."   Great sorrow prevailed
among the little community when the sad news was
received, and many tears were shed for those who had
gone, especially for the two young men, who were
loved and respected by all.

The Rev. G. H. Nobbs, Edwin's father, wrote a
hymn on the sad occasion, which was frequently sung
by the people of Norfolk Island, to the tune Jerusa
lem the Golden (Ewing).   A copy of the words and
music was sent to their friends on Pitcairn Island.
Following is the hymn, which was soon learned and
frequently sung:—

"O Lord, the heathens' madness
   Has caused our tears to flow;
Yet still, amid our sadness,
   This thought assuages woe,—
There's naught on earth progressing
   That's hidden from Thy sight,
Correcting, as in blessing
   'Shall not our God do right?'

"Our loved ones' toils are over,
   Life's transient journey sped,
Till earth her slain discover,
   And ocean yields her dead;
Then at their Lord's appearing,
   Decked with the martyrs' crown,
And spotless raiment wearing,
   Shall as His seed be known.

"We kiss the hand that smote us,
   And bow before the rod;
Thou hast in mercy taught us
   To know that Thou art God.
With undisguised submission
   We would approach Thy throne,
Presenting this petition,
   'Thy will, O Lord, be done.' "

There had been two deaths on the island since the second party arrived, and those took place within a few weeks of each other. The first was that of Hannah Young, John Adam's youngest daughter, in her sixty-third year; the other a young girl, both victims of consumption.

During the year 1867 the people had the pleasure of enjoying the visits of the royal mail steamers *Rakaia* and *Kaikoura*. The former called three times.

and the latter once, before the Panama line was broken up. The account of the *Rakaia's* first visit, written by a gentleman of the name of Dilke, who was a passenger on board, and which was published in the *Leisure Hour* for 1868 or 1869, eventually reached the island, and was read with much interest by the people. The illustration that accompanied the article caused a great deal of amusement, as it represented a canoe ornamented with cocoanut leaves and loaded with fruit, being paddled off to a vessel in the distance. The canoe had two occupants, each one clad in a small waistcloth as his only covering. The representation was not very true to fact. As a further illustration of what those in the outside world knew about the little isolated rock and the people upon it, may be told the following little incident:—

About two years before the *Rakaia's* call, a merchant vessel, the *John L. Demock*, on her passage from the Australian colonies to San Francisco, lay becalmed for two nights and a day off the island. The ship was not seen, as she came in on the south side of the island. On the second day, as the people on board saw no boat from the shore nor any other sign that the island was inhabited, they lowered a boat, and its crew, with several gentlemen passengers, pulled for the shore. The people on shore descried the boat only when she was within a short distance from land, and a canoe or two put off to meet and welcome the strangers. and show them the landing place. It was an agreeable surprise to the visitors to find themselves addressed in the English language, and the hearty welcome extended to them, and the warm invitation to come and partake of the hospitalities of the island, entirely disarmed them of their fears, and they hastily hid away the weapons of defense with which they had come well armed in case of a hostile attack.   Their stay of a day and a night was sufficient to prove that nothing but good will was felt toward them by all, and on leaving they took with them their boat loaded down with all that the island could supply.   On reaching the ship they found their companions getting ready another boat and more weapons to come in search of them, fearing that they might have fallen in with enemies.   But the long detention was happily explained, and the good ship soon was on her way again.   Some questions that have been put to those who go on board ship, even at this late date, are very amusing.   "Do you know what *that* is?" was asked of one of the islanders, the article in question being a lump of sugar. "Can you read writing?"   "Can anyone on the island read?" or, "You do not know what reading is?" and similar questions have been earnestly asked by some who for the first time have become acquainted with the people.

In March of 1868 John Buffett, now over seventy years of age, but still hale and active, came to visit his only daughter, Mrs. Mary Young.   Everybody was glad to welcome the old man, whom no one had expected to see again.   In June of the same year the *Ashburton*, from the colonies, made a call, stopping for

a day and a night. Her captain, Smith, was a former
acquaintance, and now, as a large company of passengers was with him, he kindly allowed them to come
ashore and spend the day. The ladies and gentlemen
were not slow to avail themselves of the kind permission, and the pleasure of their short visit was as much
enjoyed by the islanders as by themselves. A table
long enough for the whole party was spread, around
which they all sat down to a dinner that had been
hastily gotten up for them. In the evening some of
the company belonging to an opera troupe led by Mr.
Fred Lyster and Miss Minnie Walton, sang a few of
their songs for the entertainment of the people, and
in return the schoolchildren sang some of their part
songs. These ended, the visitors took their leave, as
night had come on, but the beautiful moon, shining in
its full brilliancy, lighted the way over the rippling
waters, as the boat, weighed down with its living
human freight, glided on its way, after the hearty
"Godspeed" had been spoken.

In July, 1872, John Buffett returned to Norfolk
Island on the whale ship *Sea Ranger*, accompanied by
one of his grandsons and another young man. They
were received by their relatives and friends on Norfolk
Island with every demonstration of joy, their unexpected arrival causing intense excitement. Every
attention was shown them, and feast and dance were
gotten up in behalf of their visitors. On receiving an
invitation to visit the pretty chapel and grounds of the
Melanesian Mission, they went, and were impressed

with the order and neatness that prevailed everywhere. The orderly behavior of the students, and the exactness which characterized the arrangements of the whole establishment, under the able management of Mr. R. H. Codrington, who was during that time at the head of the mission, called forth their highest admiration, and repeated visits only served to strengthen the impressions at first received that a noble work was being done at the mission.

The bishop of Auckland, New Zealand, was at the same time on a visit to Norfolk Island, and during his stay confirmed some of the young people, of which act he makes mention in his "Notes of a Visit to Norfolk Island," as follows:—

"November 16, Saturday. I had a class of young people from the settlement (*i. e.*, the home of the quondam Pitcairners) who were to be confirmed on the following day. . . . My class was held in St. Barnabas Chapel. Afterwards I received a visit from two young men, James Russell McCoy and Benjamin Stanley Young (brother of Fisher Young, killed at Santa Cruz in 1864), who had recently come by a whaling vessel from Pitcairn's Island. They wished to be admitted to confirmation, and I was very glad that they should be, after having some conversation with them upon the subject."

Besides the confirmation service, Bishop Cowie ordained three deacons from among the Melanesians. This ceremony was witnessed by the two young men with much interest. The service was performed in the church of the Norfolk islanders, a building which had been completed by them a short time before, and of which they were justly proud, the whole being designed and finished by themselves. It had been dedicated under the name of All Saints. Bishop Cowie's "Notes" thus make mention of the ordination service:—

"The ordination was held at eleven o'clock, morning prayer having been said for the Norfolk islanders at an earlier hour by Mr Nobbs, the chaplain of the settlement. It was at first intended to hold the ordination at St. Barnabas, but as in that case the Norfolk islanders could not have been present at the service, owing to the smallness of the mission chapel, it was thought better that the Melanesians should go down to the settlement (three miles distant), the new church there, All Saints, being large enough to hold all the church-going population of the island. . . . The venerable pastor of the quondam Pitcairn islanders, the Rev. G. H. Nobbs, assisted me at the ministration of the holy communion, . . . the communicants numbering over a hundred. Whilst the clergy were communicating, Heber's beautiful hymn, 'Bread of the world in mercy broken,' was softly and sweetly sung by the congregation. . . .

" In the afternoon at three o'clock I held a confirmation at All Saints for the Norfolk islanders. . . . The preface to the confirmation service was read by the Rev. G. H. Nobbs, whose granddaughter, Catherine Nobbs, played the harmonium accompaniment at

both the services. Twenty young people were confirmed (including the two lately arrived from Pitcairn's
Island), nearly all being descendants of the *Bounty*
mutineers. The hymns were particularly well sung
by nearly the whole congregation, one of them to the
tune Cambridge New, said to have been a great favorite
with Bishop Patteson. A son and a daughter of John
Adams, of the *Bounty*, viz., George Adams and Rachel
Evans, both over seventy years of age, were at the
service, and I went to see Arthur Quintall, now quite
imbecile, the son of another of the mutineers."

The three aged persons above mentioned were the
only survivors on Norfolk Island of the children of
the mutineers, for death had taken away many of the
people in the space of nine years. In 1868 a malignant fever swept like a blasting wind over the island,
and many of the people died, so that the two young
visitors missed the faces of many a dear relative and
friend whom they still remembered well. Several
other changes had taken place on the island. The
people had in many instances removed to their own
allotments of land, and were now living widely separated from one another.

The visit, of nearly three months' duration, was
rendered as delightful and pleasing as possible, and
they left their kind friends with feelings of hope as
well as of sorrow, for the young men had expectations
of returning again to live on the island before many
years had passed. On leaving, letters from the people
on Norfolk Island were given them to take home.

These letters contained strong advice and earnest entreaties to their friends on Pitcairn Island to return to them and live together in one community as before. Every argument that could be brought to bear on the subject was used to induce the Pitcairners to return to Norfolk Island. When the letters were, on their arrival, read to the people, and the question thoroughly discussed, the majority favored the proposal. That all obstacles should be removed, their friends had generously offered to charter and fit out a vessel at their own expense for the purpose of conveying them back to Norfolk Island, promising also that if they should return their former grants of land would be restored to them. The condition was that all should return, as otherwise they could scarcely be expected to put themselves to such an expense. Naturally, most of the younger members of the community were eager to return, and some among the older ones were not unwilling. But a few of the families were determined to remain where they were, and there the matter ended.

One argument given in favor of their return was the change that Pitcairn Island had undergone in the space of a very few years. Extreme scarcity of water was a source of much discomfort and anxiety to the inhabitants, and the soil, that had formerly been so productive, seemed now to have lost its remarkable fertility. The yam crop, which hitherto had yielded so well, and had been one of the principal food supplies, now failed almost entirely. Nor did the sweet potato escape the general plague, for a very troublesome blight would attack the young plantation, completely preventing its growth, and when the tubers became matured, they were often infested by a destructive worm, that worked untold mischief among them.

The breadfruit, too, yielded to the general decline, and splendid trees that once bent beneath their wealth of fruit, began to decay, and failed gradually to produce fruit, until they ceased almost entirely. Other fruit trees were more fortunate and did not suffer as much as the food-producing plants. Around the entire island, along the *edge*, or precipice, where once had flourished a thick growth of stunted, hardy trees, could now be seen bare, barren soil, free to be washed away by heavy rains. During this period, when the island was undergoing such a change, it was subject to frequent seasons of drought. The water supply daily diminished, and the springs that in former years had been ceaselessly flowing now dried up, with but two exceptions. Such was the condition of Pitcairn Island when the request from Norfolk Island that the community might remove thither was sent. But the conditional proposition was not accepted, and it was never again renewed.

CHAPTER XVIII.

HE closing months of 1873, and almost the entire year of 1874, was the period when, more than any other, the island suffered from the effects of drought. As ships, the only means of communication possible with the outside world, very seldom called at the island during the years that followed the arrival of both parties from Norfolk Island, the inhabitants seemed to occupy a little world entirely by themselves, and might have remained in their remote isolation for an indefinite time were it not that an unlooked-for event happened, which led to the little island's receiving much attention from many who until now had never known of its existence, and to the reviving again of the interest shown by those who in former years proved themselves true friends.

Toward the close of January, 1875, the Liverpool ship *Cornwallis*, of the firm of Balfour, Williamson & Co., homeward bound from San Francisco, came in sight.

(188)

The captain in his boyhood had read the story of the
mutineers of the *Bounty* and their subsequent settlement of the isolated rock, and decided that he would
make a call at the place where, just eighty-five years
before, Christian and his guilty party had landed.
Taking with him his apprentices, they left the ship in
charge of the first officer, and came ashore in their
own boat, accompanied by some of the island men
who had gone off to the ship.

But a very short time had elapsed after they landed
when the ship was observed to be losing her ground,
and, as if impelled by some unseen power, she drifted
shoreward, coming on swiftly and surely to destruction. The people on shore watched with breathless
anxiety and terror the doomed ship, and earnest but
unavailing prayers went up that the fearful catastrophe
might be averted. The poor captain, half frantic,
rushed with his young men and all the island men that
were within call, to the landing place, to launch the boat
and put off to the vessel, that was every moment near-
ing the rocks. But no effort could save her, and she
soon struck on some unseen rocks a few feet from the
shore. Had there been ten minutes more time, she
would have been saved, as the water clear to the shore
is very deep, and a few minutes more would have sufficed to steer the ship clear of danger.

A few of the islanders that had remained on the
ship when the boat first went off, terrified beyond
control at the approaching shipwreck, now hastily got
into their boat and started for the shore. Meeting

the captain's boat returning, they also went back to where the ship now lay, a helpless wreck. The excitement that prevailed was great, and soon everybody was near the scene of the disaster. The other men that had been engaged about their several duties when the disaster took place, now returned from the fields, and, seeing what had happened, were quickly on the rocks near where the ship lay. Swimming off to the vessel, they were soon engaged with the others who had been before them in rendering what assistance they were able, and in a short time after the ship struck, all the crew had been safely landed.

Little else was saved. The mate wished to make a return trip to the vessel in spite of the wind, that was now increasing into a gale, and at the cry, "Who will volunteer?" a ready response was given, but the darkness coming on, and the threatening weather, made it advisable to delay the effort until the next morning. The boat was once more drawn up to a place of safety, and in the gloomy darkness, with feelings still more gloomy, the captain and crew of the *Cornwallis*, accompanied by the islanders, men, women, and children, formed a silent procession up the steep hill path that led to the village. All that could be done for the strangers thus unexpectedly thrown amongst them was done as well as their limited means afforded, and everyone willingly gave up sleeping rooms to the shipwrecked men during their enforced stay, being content that their unexpected guests should enjoy whatever could be provided for their comfort.

The chief anxiety experienced was how to find enough to feed their guests should their stay be a long one, for this addition to their number was confessedly a tax upon them in the matter of food supplies, the islanders themselves being obliged to be careful in the use of what they had, as the island had not yet recovered from the effects of the long-continued drought of the previous years. Not a thing was saved from the ship. The heavy seas rolled over the poor vessel during the night, and by morning the gale had increased to such fury that it was hopeless to attempt a return to the ship, each oncoming wave threatening to overturn it or break it in pieces. The deepest sympathy was felt for the distressed captain and his company of officers and men, but nothing could be done to alleviate the misery of their condition.

On the second day after the ship had become a wreck, she turned over and broke up by the violence of the waves. The sea around was strewn with wreckage, which floated away to leeward. The ship's lifeboat, uninjured, was among the things that were scattered from the ship on breaking up, and in the hope of rescuing it a crew of the islanders started to launch the captain's gig. With brave hearts and strong arms they waited for a moment's lull in the angry waves to give them an opportunity of getting safely over the dreadful surf that rolled ceaselessly in to shore. At last the moment came, and at the command, "Pull ahead," with a strength that seemed more than human, the boat was got beyond the danger of the breakers,

that threatened to engulf her.   In due time the lifeboat was reached.   Being full of water, each man
took turns to bail the boat.   Wind and tide being both
against them, the work was exceedingly heavy, but
courageous hearts and willing hands insured success,
and after several hours' hard battling with the sea, the
gig and lifeboat were both landed in safety.

A sad accident occurred on shore while the men
were engaged in rescuing the boat.   A boy twelve
years of age had, with some of his companions, gone
down to the rocks near which the ship was wrecked,
to get something that floated ashore.   In attempting
to reach his object, he was suddenly struck down by
a heavy sea, and washed off into the boiling waters.
The only aid that could be rendered was by means of
a rope thrown to him, but before it could be brought
the poor boy had sunk, bruised and killed by the
wreckage that was tossing around.   The poor, distracted mother witnessed the fearful scene, and in her
agonizing grief made her way to the place where her
boy was taken off, and would have thrown herself into
the sea, as if such a sacrifice could avail to save her
boy, but the arms of strong men who had followed
held her back, and she was carried with great difficulty
and in an unconscious state up the rocky steep to her
home, where pitying friends received her and attended
her through the long, dreary months of illness that
followed.   The father was not present when the accident took place, so word was sent to him where he
was at work.   He was with difficulty restrained from

THE MISSION HOUSE.

casting himself into the angry sea in the remote hope of finding the body of his son, but at length submitted to be led home; nor was the body ever seen again, although a search was kept up for several days.

The American ship *Dauntless* had come in during the day, and Captain Wilbur waited until next morning, when, on learning what had taken place, he kindly offered to take the whole crew of the *Cornwallis* on his ship, and give them a passage to New York, whither he was bound. The ship was wrecked on Saturday, and by Tuesday noon all her crew had left, leaving only the poor remains of the good ship to remind the people of the sad occurrence.

The September following another shipwrecked crew was welcomed to the island. The Liverpool ship *Khandeish*, homeward bound from San Francisco, was wrecked on the reefs of Oeno Island, and the crew, taking with them what could be saved from the ship's stores, and a little of their clothing, left in their big boat and gig for Pitcairn Island. The wind favoring, the short voyage was soon accomplished. As soon as the shipwrecked mariners' boats were seen, a crew of the islanders put off in their boat—the gig that had been left by Captain Hammond, of the *Cornwallis*—to meet and welcome their unlooked-for visitors. When all had landed, the crew of the ship was divided into companies of twos and threes for their better accommodation amongst the families with whom they were to stay, and who all had gone down to the beach to receive them. They were made welcome to the

homes of the people, and were soon like members of
the families where each sojourned, taking part in the
daily labors, and joining with them in their family
worship, as well as attending all the religious services
that were held. During their stay of fifty-one days
they behaved in a way to win the approval of all, and
when, on the 19th of November, they left on the British ship *Ennerdale* for San Francisco, the parting on
both sides was expressive of much sorrow. One of
the men remained behind and was shortly afterwards
married to a widow to whom he had become attached.

The captain, officers, and crew of the *Khandeish*,
on their arrival in San Francisco, represented the condition of the Pitcairn islanders as a very needy one
indeed, although the islanders themselves, accustomed
all their lives to the simplest manner of living, did not
realize so fully as their late guests did their "forlorn
condition," as some of the papers expressed it. Of
the treatment they received while on the island they
spoke in terms of warmest gratitude, and did what
they could in return for the hospitality that had been
shown them. In this they succeeded beyond their
utmost expectations, for the generous citizens of San
Francisco responded with such heartiness that con-
tributions kept pouring in, and every useful and necessary article that was thought of,—cooking utensils,
tinware of almost every description, cups, plates,
spoons, etc., etc., wooden pails and tin pails,—testified
to their large-hearted liberality. Clothing made and
unmade, buttons, pins, needles, etc., almost enough to

stock a respectable haberdasher's shop, were contributed to the immense stock of goods collected in response to the call of charity and benevolence. A good supply of flour, a luxury to the islanders, was sent by Captain Skelly, of the *Khandeish*, as his contribution to the general stock. As a crowning gift to the whole, a beautifully-toned organ, of the Mason & Hamlin Organ Company, was sent.

The gifts came on different ships, the first part being brought by Captain D. A. Scribner, of the American ship *St. John*, which arrived at the island in March, 1876. The captain was a very dear friend of the islanders, having made repeated calls to the island before. He was intrusted with a large mail from the ship's company that had lately left the island, and whose letters were frequent in their expressions of gratitude for the kindness that had been shown them during their temporary sojourn, and were also full of praise at the munificence and generosity displayed by the good people of San Francisco, who had so willingly responded to the call for charity.

To say that the islanders were grateful for the goodness so lavishly showered upon them, would but faintly express what they really felt Grateful indeed they were, yet none the less did they feel their unworthiness that they should be the favored recipients of so much bounty in return for the small acts of human kindness rendered their fellow-men in distress, and which they rightly considered were only their duty to do.

The organ was brought by Captain Scribner. Directly on its being landed it was lifted on the shoulders of a few strong men and borne by them up the steep path, nor was the heavy but precious burden set down until they reached the little thatch-roofed church, where it was placed beside the reading table. All the inhabitants, old and young, gathered around while Captain Scribner played, "Shall We Gather at the River?" Every voice joined in the song, and when it ended, repeated expressions of thanks were given to the kind friend who brought it, and through him to the generous friends who sent the handsome gift. Tears were in many eyes as the people stood around and witnessed the substantial proofs of the kindness they were receiving. It was a new and very delightful experience to them to listen for the first time to the tones of a perfect-keyed instrument. The only other one of the kind that the island boasted was an old harmonium, that, weak-lunged and out of tune, had been given to a young woman by the doctor of H. M. S. *Petrel*, which was on a day's visit to the island two months before. The old feeble instrument had been taken to pieces and cleared from the rubbish and dust that had accumulated within it, and otherwise repaired, so that now, with its really sweet tones, it served for the young people to practice their first lessons in instrumental music, which they were not slow to do, notwithstanding the fact that they had no book or teacher to aid or direct them. And now, when the new organ was opened, all who wished had the gratification of trying a few chords on it, and enjoying the power of the instrument, an experience delightful as it was new. The donors themselves would have felt rewarded had they seen how much pure enjoyment their beautiful gift conferred, a gift that was valued with keen appreciation by everyone.

Among the many and various presents sent from San Francisco, the wants of the school were not forgotten, and a large supply of schoolbooks came— books new and old, and ranging from the first to fifth and sixth readers. This want, so generously supplied, was one of the greatest that had been experienced, and the children as well as the teacher hailed with delight the prospect of having a book all to one's self, and no longer being obliged to read from the same book turn by turn. The change was truly gratifying, for before this the school had for its best reader, speller, and grammar an old copy of Lindley Murray excepted, a few antiquated copies of good old Mavor's spelling book, dog-eared, and so literally worn out that in places here and there the words were entirely obliterated and many of the leaves had become loose and dropped out through age and usage. The one venerable copy of an old book of geography was succeeded by a goodly number of others, which opened to the children's view a world hitherto undreamed of.

It would occupy too much space to give a detailed account of everything sent to the people, every article of which was gratefully received and thoroughly appreciated. In recounting the deeds of generous kindness lavishly bestowed upon the islanders from time to time, it should never be forgotten how large a debt of gratitude they owe to their friends both in Valparaiso and Honolulu, as well as in England.   But while they were thankful for favors shown, the thought was none the less humiliating that, in their peculiar circumstances, they were obliged to be dependent upon the charity of others for some of the very necessaries of life.   Whaling ships and trading vessels, the former sources of such supplies, now ceased almost entirely to come to the island.   Had there been a way by which they could, through their own efforts, procure all that was needed for their necessities, the necessary labor would have been willingly bestowed; but their extremely isolated position rendered such efforts almost impossible.

VISIT of REAR-ADMIRAL DE HORSEY

CHAPTER XIX.

EARLY Sunday morning, on the 8th of September, 1878, the islanders were greatly surprised at seeing a British man of-war to the north of the island. As the mist and light rains that partly hid the ship from view cleared away, she was seen standing in toward the land, with the evident intention of communicating with the shore. The one boat that the islanders possessed was soon launched and on its way to the ship. After a short stay it returned, accompanied by others from the ship, which was H. M. S. *Shah*. the flagship of the admiral commanding the Pacific station. A large crowd from the ship came on shore, and as they came in time for the morning service, the still unfinished meetinghouse that was being built at the time was furnished with seats formed by boards laid across boxes, to accommodate the congregation, whose number was doubled by the addition of the visitors.

The chaplain of the ship, Rev. J. Reed, took part in

officiating. The people greatly enjoyed the pleasure
of having Admiral De Horsey and his officers join
with them in their worship and service, and would
have been pleased to have them remain through the
afternoon, but the admiral was anxious to leave on the
evening of the same day, so their stay was unavoidably
short. However, he afterward kindly yielded to the
request to remain until the next day, to afford the people opportunity to get some fruit and other things for
their visitors, as they felt that they could not consci-
entiously allow themselves to do so on the Sunday.
Having decided to prolong his stay, the admiral gave
an invitation to all the islanders to come on board at
eight the next morning to visit his ship and have
breakfast there. Most of the people availed themselves of the kind invitation and were ready at an early
hour for the anticipated pleasure. The day opened
calm and dull, with occasional light showers of rain,
which, while they dampened the garments, failed to
damp the spirits of those who visited the ship.
Breakfast was laid on a long table in the cabin, and at
the appointed hour a large party sat down with the
good admiral to partake of the bountiful feast he had
ordered.

The kind people on board seemed to vie with each
other in their efforts to entertain and please, showing
their visitors about their huge home on the waters, and
how they lived, enjoying, too, the evident wonder and
admiration displayed by their guests as they watched
the revolving of the mighty engines, and also the keen

pleasure and interest they manifested in everything they saw around them. On deck the band was playing, while in one of the rooms below one of the officers was seated at a piano, making music for a company of admiring listeners. In the gun room the crowd of young officers had gathered the schoolchildren together, and persuaded them to sing some of their songs and glees, they in return singing some of their bright, lively songs. The hours flew quickly, and soon one by one the islanders passed down the steep sides of the ship to return home, after wishing their kind visitors good-by, and carrying with them a lively remembrance of their delightful entertainment on board, while the *Shah*, with her over eight hundred souls, steamed on her way and was soon out of sight.

The following is the report of Rear Admiral de Horsey, commander in chief on the Pacific station, which was received at the admiralty:—

"September 17, 1878. Sir, I request you will acquaint the lords commissioners of the admiralty that, as Pitcairn Island lay in my track from Esquimalt to Valparaiso, and the weather being sufficiently favorable for landing, I took advantage of the circumstance to visit that island, for the purpose of ascertaining the condition of the inhabitants, and also to obtain refreshments on this long voyage. Having sighted Pitcairn at daylight on the 8th inst., we arrived at Bounty Bay at 8 A. M., and remained off the island until noon the following day, when we proceeded on our voyage.

14

"A few particulars as to the present condition of this small and almost inaccessible island, the only spot of British territory lying in the vast triangle between Vancouver, Falkland, and Fiji Islands, may not be uninteresting to their lordships, and are therefore made the subjects of this letter. The population at present numbers ninety, of all ages, of which forty-one are males and forty-nine females. . . . There is but one survivor of the generation which immediately followed the mutineers, viz., Elizabeth Young, aged about eighty-eight, daughter of John Mills, gunner's mate of the *Bounty*, and of an Otaheitian mother.

"The oldest man on the island is Thursday October Christian, grandson of Fletcher Christian, master's mate of the *Bounty*. The population may be further described as consisting of sixteen men, nineteen women, twenty-five boys, and thirty girls. The deaths on the island have numbered about twelve in the last nineteen years, as no contagious diseases visit the island. . . .

"A few medicines which were sent from Valparaiso in H. M. S. *Reindeer* (in 1869) are administered as required, by the pastor. Pitcairn Island is governed by a 'magistrate and chief ruler in subordination to her Majesty the Queen of Great Britain,' who not only administers the laws, but also enacts them. There are two councillors to advise and assist the chief magistrate, besides which, the 'heads of families' are convened for consultation when required. . . . The chief magistrate is elected annually on New Year's day, and is open to reelection. Both sexes of and

above the age of seventeen have a vote.   The office
is at present filled by Mr. James Russell McCoy, who
is also steersman of the only boat on the island.
. . .   Divine service is held every Sunday at
10:30 A. M. and at three P. M., . . . and it is
conducted strictly in accordance with the liturgy of
the Church of England, by Mr. Simon Young, their
selected pastor, who is much respected.   A Bible class
is held every Wednesday, when all who conveniently
can, attend.   There is also a general meeting for
prayer on the first Friday of every month.   Family
prayers are said in every house the first thing in the
morning and the last thing in the evening, and no food is
partaken of without asking God's blessing before and
afterwards.   Captain Beechy, writing fifty-three years
ago, says: 'These excellent people appear to live together in perfect harmony and contentment, to be
virtuous, religious, cheerful, and hospitable, to be patterns of conjugal and paternal affection, and to have
very few vices.'   I have ventured to quote those words,
as they hold true to this day, the children having followed in the footsteps of their parents.

"The observance of Sunday is very strict; no work
is done; but this is not in any pharisaical spirit, as
shown on the occasion of our visit, which chanced to
be on a Sunday, when everything consistent with not
neglecting divine service was done to supply us with
refreshments for the crew, the chief magistrate arguing
that it was a good work, and necessary, as the ship
could not wait.   Of these islanders' religious attri-

butes no one can speak without deep respect. A people whose greatest privilege and pleasure is to commune in prayer with their God, and to join in hymns of praise, and who are, moreover, cheerful, diligent, and probably freer from vice than any other community, need no priest among them. The pastor also fulfills the duty of schoolmaster, in which he is assisted by his daughter, Rosalind Amelia Young. The instruction comprises reading, writing, arithmetic, Scripture history, and geography. The girls are taught sewing and hat making as well, and the whole are taught part singing very effectively. . . . Schooling is conducted in the church house, one end of which is used as a library, open to all. English is the only language spoken or known. [And a corruption of the same.] . . .

"The Pitcairn islanders are, of course, entirely dependent upon their own resources. They grow sweet potatoes, yams, plantains, etc., and formerly plenty of breadfruit, but these are nearly all dying out. They have also beans, carrots, turnips, cabbages, and a little maize, pineapples, custard apples, and plenty of oranges, lemons, and cocoanuts. Clothing is obtained alone from passing ships in barter for refreshments. They have a few sheep, goats, pigs, fowls, cats, and dogs. As it rains generally once a month, they have plenty of water, although at times in former years they have suffered from drought. No alcoholic liquors, except for medical purposes, are used, and a drunkard is unknown. The houses are well ventilated, and furnished sufficient

GROUP OF WOMEN AND CHILDREN.

for their simple wants. Scarcely any trees good for timber grow here. . . . The men are chiefly employed tilling their grounds, farming, house building, canoe fishing, etc.; the women, in sewing, hat and basket making (in addition to their other household work). All are industrious, and willing to take their share of public work when required. This, at present, is enlarging the church house, to meet the wants of an increasing population.

"The only communication with the outside world is by means of passing ships, averaging perhaps one a month, and chiefly those on their way to and from California; but this is precarious, as most ships fetch to windward of Pitcairn, and those that do sight the island are frequently unable to communicate. At the time of our visit the landing was considered good, but it was necessary to watch for a smooth place, and to use a light boat. They have no communication with Otaheite, and very rarely with Norfolk Island or New Zealand.

"The necessary articles required by the islanders are best shown by those we furnished in barter for refreshments, viz., flannel, serge, drill, half boots, combs, tobacco, and soap. They also stand much in need of maps and slates for their school, and tools of any kind are most acceptable. I caused them to be supplied from the public stores with a Union Jack for display on ships' arrival, and a pit saw, of which they were greatly in need. This, I trust, will meet the approval of their lordships. If the munificent people of England were only aware of the wants of this most deserving little colony, they would not go long unsupplied. I would suggest that anything desired to be sent be addressed to the care of the admiral on this station, either at Coquimbo or Vancouver Island. If sent by private ships, goods may never reach the island. Within the last two years or so two wrecks have occurred—the English ship *Khandeish*, on Oeno Island, and the English ship *Cornwallis*, on Pitcairn Island. In both cases the crews took refuge on Pitcairn Island, remaining respectively over six weeks and three days, and receiving every assistance, including food and clothing, from the scanty supplies of the Pitcairn islanders. At the wreck of the *Cornwallis* the islanders in rendering assistance lost their only boat, one made by themselves, and thus their only means of communicating with passing ships. . . .

"One stranger, an American, has settled on the island—a doubtful acquisition. A few of the islanders have expressed a wish to return to Norfolk Island —a not unnatural wish for change—but the chief magistrate thinks none are likely to go. The islanders, at my invitation, visited the *Shah*. No less than sixty-eight men, women, and children, out of a total of ninety, came on board, regardless of the difficulties of embarking, and the wind and rain. Their poor garments were nearly wet through, and many were seasick, but the pleasure of going on board one of their own country's ships of war outweighed all other considerations, and made them essentially happy.

"Finally I submit to their lordships that when the service will admit it is desirable that a ship of war should visit Pitcairn annually, and I propose to cause this to be done during the remainder of my command. I submit also that this small colony is deserving such attention and encouragement as Her Majesty's government may think fit to hold out to it. Her Majesty the Queen does not, I believe, possess in any part of the world more loyal and affectionate subjects than this little knot of settlers. I may here observe that a notion appears to prevail among the Pitcairn islanders that Her Majesty's government is displeased with them for having returned from Norfolk Island (which, as their lordships are aware, they did in two parties, the first in 1859 and the rest, I believe, in 1864), although their return was, I believe, at their own expense, and they have since been no burden to the Crown. This notion, whence received I know not, I venture to affirm was without foundation, feeling assured that Her Majesty's government would rather honor them for preferring the primitive simplicity of their native island to either the dissolute manners of Otaheite or even the more civilized but less pure and simple ways of Norfolk Island. . . . They will lose rather than gain by contact with other communities. I have etc., etc.   A. F. R. DE HORSEY,
"*Rear Admiral and Commander in Chief.*"

In July, 1879, the year following the visit of the *Shah*, H. M. S. *Opal* came, bringing a beautiful organ of American manufacture—Clough & Warren's

—as a gift from the Queen, Her Majesty having sent the sum of £20 to Admiral de Horsey for the benefit of the Pitcairn islanders. This he expended in the purchase of the above-named gift, thinking, and rightly too, that the money could not be spent in a more satisfactory way. The organ is ornamented with a heart-shaped silver plate placed in the center above the keyboard, bearing the inscription, "A present from Her Majesty the Queen to her loyal and loving Pitcairn Island subjects, in appreciation of their domestic virtues." This gift was received with pardonable pride that the Queen should condescend to remember the little isolated colony, as well as with feelings of true loyalty toward, and love for, their sovereign. When the captain of the *Opal* seated himself at the instrument and struck a few chords of the national song of Great Britain, there was not a voice that did not join heartily in singing, "God save the Queen."

Besides the organ, the result that immediately followed the admiral's appeal to the "munificent people of England" was seen in the abundant and varied substantial gifts sent to the island on H. M. S. *Osprey* in March, 1880. When the admiral's account of his visit was published in England, a ready response was made to his appeal by many friends there, and subscriptions were immediately set on foot. The chairman of the committee to direct matters and dispose of the various subscriptions, the Rev. Andrew A. W. Drew, a clergyman of the Church of England, par-

ticularly exerted himself in the interests of the islanders, he and his wife attending personally to the pack-
ing of the many boxes that contained the gifts, the
task being a most wearisome one, as, owing to the long
way the boxes had to come, they needed to be packed
with the greatest care.   Every article that was sent
was of the best.   A large supply of schoolbooks and
the much-needed slates and pencils also came, a gratefully received addition to what the good people of San
Francisco had previously supplied.   Especial mention
should be made of the handsome gift of a number of
Oxford Bibles—teachers' editions and others.   Each
Sunday school teacher was furnished with a teacher's
Bible, which was valued accordingly, and the happy
possessors felt that on them were bestowed the richest
gifts that England sent.

The beautiful and costly present of two boats was
also received, and that too with feelings akin to shame
that so much thought and kindness had been bestowed
on the islanders, whose part in receiving far surpassed
that of the "more blessed" giving.   One of the boats
was named "Queen Victoria," and it bears an inscription to the effect that it was a gift sent in recognition
of the "gallant services rendered by the islanders in
saving life."   The other boat, a whaleboat, was named
"Admiral Drew," in remembrance of the father of the
Rev. A. Drew, the gentleman above mentioned.   Mr.
Drew had had the latter boat built strictly in accordance with his own directions, and the beautiful little
craft answers admirably the purpose for which it was

intended, viz., battling with the heavy surf that so
frequently beats upon the shore.

Thus much in regard to the response made to the
admiral's appeal by the large-hearted donors in England. A volume could, however, be written respecting the numberless gifts from private individuals and
others, that have from time to time been showered
upon the people of this remote spot of earth, gifts
that have been received with gratitude mingled with
a feeling of unworthiness on the one hand, and of
dependence on the other, enabling the recipients to
experience in all its force the truth of the expression,
"It is more blessed to give than to receive."

An attempt had been made two years previous, by
a firm in Liverpool, De Wolfe & Co., to establish some
sort of business on the island, the planting and raising
of cotton, preparing cocoanut and candlenut, and
also arrowroot, by these means to enable them to
supply their simple wants through their own exertions. But the little island was too far removed from
any business center to make it a paying concern, and
in less than two years after the attempt was made it
was broken up.

FRIENDLY VISITS

CHAPTER XX.

ABOUT the middle of the year 1880 seven of the youth from Norfolk Island came on a visit to the old home of their parents. Scarcely any communication passed between the two islands, so that the event of their coming was improved in learning all about the state of the island and people they had lately left.

The friends of the young men noticed with surprise that, with but one exception, they were all slaves to the tobacco habit, both chewing and smoking, for not one among the youth of the island practiced the unclean vice. The captain of the whale ship with whom they had come was himself a total abstainer as regarded both tobacco and spirits, but all his endeavors to reform the young men under his command, example and precept notwithstanding, failed to have the desired effect. He was more successful when he attempted a reform among the old men of the island, in one case at least, as the following incident will show.

In a meeting held on Sunday evening the captain

addressed himself to the tobacco users, seven in number, and those, five at least, the oldest men in the community.   He spoke very strongly against the bad habit to which they were addicted, and its consequent evil results.   Some of his hearers were for the moment impressed with his appeals, and two of them almost decided to abandon the vice forever.   They respected their would-be reformer enough not to indulge in the practice in his presence.   On the following morning, as one of the men was walking along the road with a lighted pipe in his mouth, he espied the captain a few yards ahead of him, waiting to give him a warm morning greeting.   Regardless of the consequences, in the fear of being found out, he quickly caught the heated clay pipe from his lips and thrust it into his pocket, which was as quickly burnt through.   Though smarting with the pain, he bravely shook hands with the captain and passed on, not daring to betray his pipe, even at the cost of suffering.   But it was the last struggle he had with the habit, for from that day it was abandoned, and he was made free, yet "so as by fire."

It was during this same year, 1880, that an unusual and very peculiar visitation appeared among the community, affecting only the younger members, eleven or twelve young persons in all having been subject to it. The disease, if such it may be called, was temporary insanity, the case that lasted the longest not extending over two years.   The first symptom of the attack was a strange hallucination of the mind, the person affected seeing some object which greatly terrified him, or hearing voices calling to him, then gradually losing all recollection of former events, until the mind became an utter blank. One peculiar feature of the disease was a distorted vision, that transformed every object into something different to what it was, as, for

GIRLS IN BATHING COSTUME.

instance, a full-grown man or woman appeared as but a child, while a mere baby would assume the full proportions of a man. In almost every case the patient was calm and quiet; the power of speech seemed taken away, while the vacant stare showed that the mind had lost control over itself.

One case was that of a youth who had been ship-wrecked, and whose stay was prolonged on the island. This was in 1881. One morning he declared that during the night he saw his mother's coffin pass above him out of the window, and nothing could persuade him that it was a delusion. A few hours afterwards he became oblivious to everything that was going on around him, and in the very first stage of the disease was entirely deprived of the power of speech. When speech returned after a few days, he employed himself searching from house to house for some fancied friend who was unjustly condemned to prison, and whom he was sparing no effort to release. On one occasion he wandered away during the night to the opposite side of the island, where he was found by a party who went in search, sleeping under an over-hanging rock, wrapped up in his scout's blanket, for at that stage of his derangement he declared that he was Davy Crockett out on an Indian trail. Davy Crockett was only one out of the many different characters whom he personated in the different stages of the disease.

Many and various were the phases that the disease assumed, each patient being acted upon in a different manner. There has never been any satisfactory explanation of the cause that produced it. The case above mentioned as being of longest duration was that of a young girl whose mind became affected in April, 1884, and was restored in the early part of the year 1886. Since that time the peculiar disease has not made its appearance.

In the early part of 1881 two young men left the island to venture for the first time as far as England. There every kindness that could be shown them was bestowed. One of them, however, almost immediately on landing, was secured as a highly prized specimen of the human species, to be exhibited in the Westminster Aquarium. Entirely ignorant of the intention of the parties who had obtained him, he consented to their proposal to accompany them, and they were soon speeding away from Liverpool to London, where he was duly settled in his place in the aquarium, and advertised. "Does he eat like other people?" was one of the many questions that amused him, as it was earnestly put by one of the spectators. A bluff old sea captain was very indignant that he had to pay for the privilege of seeing an old acquaintance whom he had twice visited in his far-away island home.

But he was not kept long in his unenviable position, for the Rev. A. W. Drew, a clergyman of the Church of England, no sooner learned of the facts of the case than he immediately came to the rescue. He at once had the visitor from Pitcairn Island, whose health was much impaired, removed to his own home, where he was taken care of and waited upon in his hours of weakness and suffering with every attention and care that kindness and love could suggest. Even when his life was all but despaired of, the good clergyman and his estimable wife never gave up their hope and trust in God that He would bless the efforts that were made to restore their guest to health again. Their house

15

was his home during the rest of his stay, and the unwearying love and care manifested by the many friends who came to see him, as well as by the clergyman and his family, made an impression upon his mind that could never be effaced.   The other visitor shared the same kindness and attention that were so lavishly bestowed upon his companion, the worthy people of Hull, to which port his ship went, doing all that lay in their power for him while he stayed with them.   On their arrival in San Francisco they experienced everywhere they went the utmost favors that thoughtfulness could suggest or friendship could show.

In June of the same year another of the young men from the island left for England.   The two who preceded him returned home after an absence of one year and two years respectively, but the third, Richard Young, never came back, and after a period of nine years' absence, died in Oakland, California.

In the meantime another shipwrecked crew had been thrown upon the hospitality of the islanders. The English ship *Acadia*, outward bound from San Francisco, in about a month from leaving that port, was wrecked on Ducie Island.   As soon as it was ascertained that the ship could not be saved, preparations were made to abandon her.   The crew were able to save a considerable portion of their clothes, and, putting into their two boats as much provision as they could safely carry, made sail for Pitcairn Island, stopping for a day at Elizabeth Island.   On leaving the ship, one of their number, the boatswain, received the untimely discharge of a pistol in his body, which fortunately did not prove serious.

On leaving Elizabeth Island, the wind, being in their favor, enabled them to make a speedy passage to the place whither they were bound, and on the morning of the second day the shipwrecked mariners were gladdened by the sight of the English flag hoisted on the high peak above the landing place. As before, the men were taken in by the different families, in twos and threes, until they should have an opportunity to leave. This soon occurred, Captain George, the first officer, Mr. John Simpson, and two or three of the lads that were with them on the *Acadia*, leaving on the American ship *Edward O'Brien*, for England.

It may not be out of place to say here that, the trial that awaited them having terminated favorably, Captain George and Mr. Simpson each accepted a berth on board the steamer *Escambia*, the former occupying the position of first officer, and Mr. Simpson a grade lower. The *Escambia* left London for China, going thence to San Francisco, where, after loading, an attempt was made to put to sea before the cargo had been properly adjusted. This imprudent act ended disastrously, for the vessel keeled over and sank in a few minutes. Most of those on board went down with the ship, and amongst those who thus perished were the late captain and mate of the ill-fated *Acadia*. Of the rest of the crew left on the island, three took passage for England on the American ship *Alfred D. Snow*, and, later on, the remainder returned to San Francisco, with the exception of three, who chose to remain on the island, and a youth, whose home and parents were in San Francisco, but who had been unfairly left behind. Nor did he have an opportunity to return home until after a nine months' stay on the island.

Two of the men whose choice was to remain were after a while married, one making his home on the island, while the other, after a stay of three years, left with wife and two little children for his home in Wales, where the wife and mother died in less than a year.

The third, the carpenter of the ship, had also decided to follow his two shipmates' example, and succeeded, not wisely but too well, in winning the affections of a girl who was shortly to be married to one of the island men. But the unfortunate attachment ended unhappily, for some of the young woman's relatives, indignant at the turn of affairs, set themselves to put the matter right, according to their judgment, and enlisted the sympathies of the magistrate in their favor. He soon had an opportunity, from a fancied insult to himself, to order the Englishman off the island. The act, unjust in itself, was carried out, and he left the island on the British man-of-war *Sappho*, in July, 1882. Captain Clark, of the *Sappho*, did not conceal his opinion of the whole proceedings, but openly declared the injustice of the act. However, in accordance with the magistrate's strongly expressed wish, he received the carpenter on board his ship, and gave him a passage to Honolulu, where he obtained suitable employment.

In letters received from him he denounced bitterly and in unsparing terms all who had shared in the unworthy strife that ended in his being sent away. Before leaving, Captain Clark, by special request, framed a law which forbade henceforth the marriage of a stranger to any of the islanders, with the intention of settling amongst them. Several reasons were given why such a law should be made, the principal one being that the population was increasing quite rapidly enough without any addition from the outside. The law was afterwards amended by a clause stating that should anyone whose stay could benefit the island, wish to settle there, he might do so. But as the island offered no inducement whatever to anyone outside of its own inhabitants as a desirable place for a home, there was no danger of any addition to the population from outsiders, and the law might have remained as it was originally written.

CHAPTER XXI.

TWO years had passed away after the crew of the *Acadia* found a haven on Pitcairn Island, when one night, the 23d of August, 1883, as the islanders were about to retire to rest, they were startled by shouts and the blowing of a fog horn from over the waters. That another shipwreck had occurred somewhere near was evident, and the men, hastily mustering, went forth with lanterns into the night, and were soon at the landing place. Having launched a boat, a few minutes' rapid pulling brought them to the object of their search. It proved to be a boat which had belonged to the bark *Oregon*, now a wreck on the reefs of Oeno. She had been about a month out from Oregon on her way to Chile when she struck on the reefs that surrounded the low-lying island of Oeno. All the crew, and three passengers, a widowed lady and her two infant boys,

landed safely on Oeno Island. The position of the
ship after she struck was such as to enable the crew
to remove everything they wanted, so that they were
comfortably settled during their enforced stay.

When all had been made as comfortable as circumstances permitted, the captain, Hardy by name, and his
mate, Mr. Walker, after consulting together, decided
that the captain should take their small boat and seek
a passage through the heavy surf that broke continu-
ously on the reef surrounding the lagoon, and should
he succeed in accomplishing it safely, the rest were to
follow in the two other boats, with as much of the
goods as they could prudently carry. Captain Hardy,
accompanied by one of the sailors and the cook, left
the shore. Just when the boat had passed beyond
the smooth waters of the lagoon out into the breakers, it capsized, and the poor captain was drowned.
The mate's boat, following almost directly, passed
safely through the rolling surf, and in passing, the two
men who were clinging to the upturned boat, were res-
cued. With this addition to his crew, the mate, not
returning to tell those behind of the captain's fate, at
once steered in the direction of Pitcairn Island. The
weather being fair and the wind favorable, they reached
their destined place on the second night out.

Most of the men in the mate's boat were Chileans,
and were scarcely able to speak any word in the English language. All were received and sheltered, a
disused little building having been fitted up for their
accommodation, and after a rest of two nights and a

day Mr. Walker, leaving his own men behind, took a crew of the islanders and returned to Oeno, in search of the remainder of the ship's company. But these had not waited his return, for, having been left without a word as to what had occurred after the captain's futile attempt to effect a passage, they had launched their big boat, and, placing therein the trunks belonging to the lady, Mrs. Collyer, who, with her children, accompanied them, they too followed the way that the rest had taken. A big Irish sailor took command of the boat and found some difficulty in managing the rest of the men who were with him, and who certainly showed no disposition to willingly obey his orders. Though he possessed very limited knowledge in the art of navigation, yet, under the guidance of a merciful Providence, their boat came in all right, and the day after the mate had gone, the crew of tired men, who had rowed almost the whole distance, beheld, with a feeling of true thankfulness, the sight of land and the prospect of rest. The poor woman, too, was worn out with anxiety, and the care and attention bestowed on her when she arrived in the midst of friends were most gratifying.

Hers had been a sad experience. Her husband, the Rev. J. W. Collyer, whose field of labor had been in Chile, was going, for the benefit of his health, on a visit to his mother in the United States, and had engaged a passage for himself and family on the bark *Oregon*, for the State of the same name. Only a few days out from the South American Coast his

sickness took a sudden turn for the worse, and unexpectedly and with but a few minutes' warning he died,
leaving not one word to comfort and cheer his almost
broken-hearted wife. She had to endure the further
pain of having him buried at sea, and in her widowed
state, among strangers, she made the voyage to Oregon. She was now returning to her father's house in
Lola, Chile, when the unlooked-for disaster happened,
depriving her of the hope of soon seeing her family
and friends. But their stay on the island was of short
duration, for, ere the return of Mr. Walker from Oeno,
all had been again received on board the British ship
Leicester Castle, in command of Captain Boag, on his
way to San Francisco.

Arriving at Oeno Mr. Walker's first care was to
secure the lady's box of jewelry, which he guarded
with jealous care, but reached Pitcairn just an hour
too late to deliver the box into the lady's own hands,
as the *Leicester Castle* was about to make sail when
the mate's boat appeared, the islanders having supplied whatever they could spare from their own
slender stock of provisions to help the heavy demands
made upon the stores of the *Leicester Castle* by the
addition of a whole crew of shipwrecked men. After
a long and tedious passage Captain Boag at length
arrived in port, where the crew of the late *Oregon* were
speedily discharged. Mrs. Collyer also left almost
immediately for home, where she arrived safely in due
time, and where her box of treasures reached her
after a few months' delay. On his arrival in England

Captain Boag suffered some inconvenience on account of his having taken so many of the shipwrecked men on board his ship, and drawing so heavily on his own limited resources to supply their wants.

On the 6th of November the last survivor of the generation immediately succeeding the mutineers passed away. Elizabeth Young, *nee* Mills, and whose first husband was a son of Quintall the mutineer, died at the ripe age of ninety-three. Her struggles with the last enemy were protracted, as if life was so hard to yield up. While speech lasted, she seemed to live over again the days when, as a child, she was instructed by John Adams, and while tossing about on her bed and during her calmer moments, she never ceased repeating the prayer that John Adams taught his youthful flock to repeat before retiring to rest: "I will lay me down in peace and take my rest, for Thou, Lord, only makest me to dwell in safety. Into Thy hands I commend my body, soul, and spirit. Thou has redeemed me, O Lord, Thou God of truth." The second year following the death of old Elizabeth Young—called by everybody "ma-ma"—saw more deaths than had happened in any previous year since the island was reinhabited, four deaths occurring among the community during the year 1885.

ARRIVAL of MR. JOHN I. TAY

CHAPTER XXII.

WING to the extremely isolated situation of Pitcairn Island, and the uncertainty that attends every effort to reach it again should one venture beyond its narrow limits, the islanders had hitherto, with very few exceptions, been satisfied to spend all their lives together, rather than run the risk of leaving their lone island home without having an idea when they would see it again. In a period of twenty-seven years only five had left the island to visit other places, all being men; but in January, 1886, for the first time an island woman left her home and family, to begin life anew in a distant land. To leave behind and forever the scenes of earlier years, the fond parents and brothers and sisters, and the old life of simple duties and pleasures, to enter upon a scene of life new and untried—indeed, scarcely dreamed of— needed great courage. This she displayed, being guided by her high sense of the duty she owed her husband, who, after a stay of five years and a half, was about to return to his native land.

(229)

The pain of parting from parents, whose tender love had watched over her whole life, and from brothers, sisters, and friends who cherished her, and who prized her love and friendship, was bravely borne. Only a short time, less than a day, was allowed them in making preparations for their departure, and when the hour of parting came, the procession that followed them to the landing place was like that of a funeral, as all knew that the separation would be final. In less than a year after reaching her new home she passed away, the cold winter in a foreign land proving too severe for a constitution always delicate.

In October of the same year, 1886, on the eighteenth day of the month, there arrived the British man-of-war *Pelican,* whose captain had courteously and kindly received on board, at Tahiti, an American missionary, John I. Tay by name, a member of the body of Christians known as Seventh-day Adventists. Wishing to reach Pitcairn Island for the purpose of setting before the people what he believed were truths hitherto unknown to them, he found passage, as before stated, on board the *Pelican*. He was treated by all the officers and men with the greatest consideration and courtesy, and was successful, during the passage, in awakening sufficient interest among some of the ship's company to lead them to inquire and search further into the subjects presented in the books they received from him.

As no objection was raised by the people in regard to the question whether the missionary would be

HATTIE ANDRE'S CLASS.

allowed to stay, he was left on the island when the *Pelican* went away. Ten years earlier a large package of Seventh-day Adventist publications had been sent to the island, accompanied by letters from two of the leading ministers of that body, Elders James White and J. N. Loughborough, earnestly requesting the people to give a candid, careful reading to what had been sent them. The letters were read, but the pamphlets and tracts were regarded with suspicion, and their contents were examined very cautiously at first.

Further study awakened deeper interest, until to the minds of four-fifths of the people there came the conviction that the statements regarding the Sabbath, supported by an array of proofs from the Bible itself, were too convincing to be longer denied. Yet no one, until the coming of Mr. Tay, left Sunday keeping and accepted the seventh day as the Sabbath. This was done the second week of the missionary's stay, and before Mr. Tay left the whole community was observing and thoroughly believing in the seventh day as the Sabbath of the Lord.

A careful study of the different points of doctrine held by Seventh-day Adventists, led first to a conviction on the part of the people that their positions were correct, and finally to their acceptance of them, although they felt that this would be a matter of regret, if not of positive displeasure, to many who had hitherto expressed, and shown in a most substantial manner, the warm interest they had always felt in the island of Pitcairn and its people. While this to the islanders was sad to contemplate, they felt that they could not do otherwise than follow their convictions of duty.

After the departure of Mr. Tay, who left in the last week of November, 1886, some differences arose in regard to the manner of worship, and in the interests of harmony and Christian union a meeting was convened to talk over and consider the matter and adopt some plan of worship in which all could unite. This was in March, 1887, and the result of the meeting was that the Book of Common Prayer was laid aside.

For a year the islanders had been observing the seventh day as the Sabbath, and it was a question with them how the change would be accepted by the representatives of the British Government, under whose protection they were, when a man-of-war should arrive. Therefore, some little concern was felt when, in December, 1887, H. M. S. *Cormorant* came. The day was Sunday, and the visitors, noticing the fact that the day was not being kept as a sacred time, were curious to know the reason why. One question followed another, until the whole story was told. Perhaps the following extract from an English periodical, written by one of the gentlemen on board the *Cormorant*, best tells how the change was regarded. After a brief description of the island and how it was peopled, the writer goes on to say :—

"It will be a matter of regret, therefore, to many who are interested in the little community to hear that

within the last year or two their principles have undergone a revolution, and that they have enrolled themselves among the Seventh-day Adventists—a sect orig-
inating in the United States.   It was with natural surprise that I heard of this change, and, in the course of
conversation, found that its cause was a visit to the
island of an Adventist missionary who remained some
weeks, inculcating the doctrines of his sect among the
islanders.   He could have found no better soil in which
to sow his doubtful seed.   Very earnest and anxious
to learn, implicit believers and reverencers of the Bible,
the simple islanders, ignorant of sophistry and the
subtleties of scriptural deductions, listened attentively
to the arguments of their fanatical visitor, who, taking
the Bible as his standpoint, soon convinced them of
the soundness of his views.   .   .   .   The island was
flooded with Seventh-day Adventist literature, emanat-
ing from the headquarters of the sect in Michigan, and
the islanders were full of the enthusiasm of converts
in the pursuit of their new creed."

The article from which the foregoing extract was
taken, concludes with a very pleasing description of
the writer's feelings on awaking in the morning and
hearing the voice of praise and prayer ascending from
more than one family altar, a custom begun by John
Adams, the converted mutineer, and which continues
still.

The visit of the *Cormorant* will always be among
the bright and pleasant remembrances of the island,
although she stayed only two days.   On the first day

16

every youth and child, as well as many adults, under-
went the light operation of being vaccinated. The
act was in itself simple enough, but the virus used
was so powerful that many of those who had for the
first time been inoculated, were for several days utterly
prostrated with severe headaches and shooting pains
throughout the whole body. In many cases the
wounds showed a strong disinclination to heal, and so
great was the flow of pus that it necessitated the constant use of bandages until the lengthy process of
healing was accomplished.

Captain Nicolls gave an invitation to all who so
wished to visit his ship and enjoy a pleasant entertainment on board. The after part of the deck had been
prepared for the entertainment, and from side to side
of the ship was a great display of bunting, prettily
festooned to form a partition. The captain presided
at a large piano, while at his side stood one of his
officers, accompanying on the violin, which instrument
contributed largely to the music, two or three more
being skillfully played by as many of the ship's company. The loud cheers that greeted every fresh performance were heard on shore, and when the first star
of evening appeared, the islanders sang for their closing piece, "Twilight Is Stealing over the Sea." Then
all rose to finish the evening's enjoyment by singing
"God Save the Queen," after which the island boats,
with their human freight, started homewards, and the
Cormorant steamed away to her destination, bidding
good-by with her siren whistle.

THE MISSIONARY SHIP PITCAIRN

CHAPTER XXIII.

ON January of 1889 one of the saddest accidents that ever happened on the island occurred. A young man twenty-four years of age went out one day to search amongst the rocks for young sea birds. He was accompanied by two of his younger brothers, who held a rope, while he descended to a very dangerous place in the rocks. His brothers urged him in vain not to go, but no amount of persuasion would avail, and he pursued his purpose. He had taken a few birds and was about to try to get another a few feet above him in a small hollow in the rock, when he lost his footing and fell several hundred feet into the pitiless sea below. Breathless with haste and pale with horror, the two other boys came back to tell the awful story of what had taken place. The horror felt by everyone was great, and the piercing

(237)

cries of the mother and the wife of the young man rent the air as they ran toward the scene of the fearful accident. In as short a time as possible a boat was manned and pulled by arms nerved to their utmost strength to the spot where the young man's body fell into the water. But nothing came of the search, although it was kept up for days. All that was ever found was a hat belonging to him, and which had floated a long distance from the place where he fell.

Toward the middle of the same year an excitement of a different character was experienced. When the *Cormorant* visited the island in 1887, which was the year of the Queen's Jubilee, the captain and officers inquired whether the little community had contributed anything toward a celebration of the event. When the answer was given in the negative, they said that the Queen would acknowledge a gift, however small. Being thus encouraged, a box containing some specimens of the people's handiwork was put up as soon as possible, and sent to their sovereign.

Her Majesty was graciously pleased to receive the humble token of loyalty and love, and sent an acknowledgment, accompanied by a gift of the coins struck on the occasion of her Jubilee, varying in value from a sixpenny piece to four shilling pieces. These were to be distributed among the women and girls, and Captain Nicolls, of the *Cormorant,* on his second visit, had the pleasant duty of distributing the gift, which the receivers were proud to get and keep in remembrance of their beloved Queen. The ceremony over

the *Cormorant* left, but before the return voyage was
half accomplished, Captain Nicolls, at Rio Janeiro,
took the yellow fever and died.   He was buried at sea.

A new decade was now entered upon, and in the
opening month of 1890 the people celebrated, on the
twenty-third day, the century of years since the *Bounty*
arrived at the island.   The same period of time which
among the nations of the earth had witnessed the
amazing onward march in progress and advanced civilization, saw but little change in this little world situ-
ated by itself in the midst of the vast ocean.   Yet the
people felt that God had led them all the way, and
they met together at the church to hold a service of
praise with which to begin the day, thanking God for
past mercies and praying him to supply future grace.
Following is a hymn composed and sung on the occa-
sion·—

> Our Father, God, we come to raise
> Our songs to thee in grateful praise;
> We come to sing thy guiding hand,
> By which supported still we stand.
>
> To this fair land our fathers sought
> To flee the doom their sins had brought,
> In vain—nor peace nor rest was found,
> For strife possessed th' unhallowed ground.
>
> Darkness around their path was spread;
> Their crimes deserved a vengeance dread;
> When, lo! a beam of hope was given
> To guide their erring feet to heaven.
>
> Thy holy word, a beacon light,
> Had pierced the shades of sin's dark night,
> And poured a flood of radiance where
> Had reigned the gloom of dull despair.

We own the depths of sin and shame,
Of guilt and crime from which we came;
Thy hand upheld us from despair,
Else we had sunk in darkness there.

We, their descendants, here to-day
Meet in thy house to praise and pray,
And ask thy blessing to attend
And guide us to life's journey's end.

Oh, that our lives henceforth may be
More consecrated, Lord, to thee!
Thy boundless favors to us shown
With gratitude we humbly own.

Thou know'st the depths from whence we sprung;
Inspire each heart, unloose each tongue,
That all our powers may join to bless
The Lord, our Strength and Righteousness.

In the early part of this year, 1890, the news came
that the much-talked-of missionary schooner had been
built and would shortly sail on its mission to the
Pacific islands; but not until the 25th of November
of the same year did she arrive, making Pitcairn Island
her first stopping place. The missionaries, who were
Elders Gates and Read and their wives and Mr. and
Mrs. Tay, were gladly welcomed. After a short rest
they began the work of organizing the church and
Sabbath school. The rite of baptism was performed,
whereby all the adult members of the community were
received into the body of the church. This solemn
and impressive service was witnessed for the first time
by the people, who had hitherto seen and known only
the sprinkling of water on the faces of infants.

When the *Pitcairn*, for so the ship was named, left the island, three of the islanders went away to engage in work in different places. On her return, in July, 1892, two of her company were missing. Mr. Tay, whose name was so closely associated with the ship, and also with the island, had died at Suva, in Fiji, and the captain, Mr. Marsh, had fallen a victim to the influenza, and died in Auckland, New Zealand.

Elder Gates and his wife remained on the island, while the *Pitcairn* returned to California. Too much cannot be said of the good that their stay accomplished. Although, physically, the gentleman was not strong, he made every effort to elevate the minds of the people, who naturally had, owing to their isolated situation, very narrow and limited views of life. As soon as possible he started a class, which all the young people attended, and, to further help them, organized a literary society of over forty, in which every member took part, and which was thoroughly enjoyed as long as it was kept up.

Four months after his coming he started a paper, giving it the name of the *Monthly Pitcairnian*, to whose *written* pages all were invited to contribute. The paper had its own staff of reporters, six in number, who almost invariably failed to send in any news; nevertheless, its pages were always full. There was, first, the opening page, on which generally appeared an original poem. This was followed by the editorial page, which the editor, Elder Gates, contrived to fill with some lively article. The rest of the paper con-

sisted of five other departments, devoted to Moral and
Religious Topics, the Home Circle, News Items,
Pleasantries, and All Sorts.

On the 18th of February, 1893, the *Pitcairn* came
the second time from San Francisco, bringing, in addition to the other passengers, missionaries to be located
on different islands. A teacher from America, Miss
Hattie Andre, just graduated from college, came to
organize and teach school on Pitcairn Island. After
the necessary delay incident on a fresh arrival, immediate steps were taken to have the school fairly started.
This was done in the early part of April, and the
young people, fully aware of their lack of education,
were not slow to avail themselves of the advantages
offered them in having for their instructor one so well
qualified and fitted for the work. Forty-two young
persons, varying in age from fourteen to thirty nine
years, had their names entered as students, one of these
being a girl from Mangareva, whose two younger
brothers were placed among the other children from
the age of seven to thirteen years. These were
twenty in number, and were taught by one of the
island women.

Mrs. Gates at the same time opened a kindergarten
school for the youngest children, and had a class of
fourteen to begin with. In addition to this she organized a mothers' meeting, and had a class twice a month,
to instruct in the methods of giving treatment to the
sick, and also in cooking. Besides this she taught, or
rather attempted to teach, stenography to a few of the

young people, some of whom soon gave up the attempt
to learn.   Four diligently practiced, and were meeting
with a fair measure of success when the class was
unavoidably broken up.

The literary society and the classes taught by
Elder Gates were merged into the school, and the
Monthly Pitcairnian passed over into the hands of the
students, who were expected to keep its columns well
supplied, notwithstanding the lack of material to supply
them with.

And now is drawing near a time unparalleled in the
history of Pitcairn Island—a time when she passed
under a visitation so terrible while it lasted, and so
awful in its effects, that it was remarked that those
who survived it were not the same persons they were
before it came.   But this is anticipating.   On the 27th
of April, 1893, the shipwrecked crew of the *Bowdon*,
lost on Oeno reef, came to Pitcairn Island.   The
captain and a few others soon went away on an American ship for England, while the rest waited for an
opportunity to go back to San Francisco.   It is not
necessary to give a detailed account of their stay, but
it brought no blessing to the island.

Several trips were made to and from the wreck by
the islanders, and even several of the women accompanied their husbands and brothers in their last trip in
open boats to Oeno.   All returned in safety, no accident having occurred either going or returning, as the
weather continued fine.   This was in June, the month
of vacation.   The month following H. M. S. *Hyacinth*

came, and during her short stay several cases of sickness were attended by the doctor, who pronounced the disease to be a form of *la grippe*. Some of the persons who were suffering at that time had their lives despaired of, but all of them eventually recovered.

That the awful fever that attacked the people was introduced with the shipwrecked crew was evident. When the *Hyacinth* left, a slight attack of influenza spread among the people, aggravating the more serious disease. Everything that was possible to be done under the circumstances was accomplished, the missionaries exerting themselves to the utmost to help the stricken people, who one by one rapidly fell victims to the dread sickness. On the 26th of August the first death occurred, opening the way for many others, and before the terrible work of death was ended, twelve persons were taken away, the last death occurring on the 19th of October. So urgent were the calls for help from those who were helpless that there was scarcely time to weep for the dead, and the few who passed unstricken through the fiery ordeal were constant in their attendance, night and day, until nature itself nearly gave up the struggle.

Some of the most valued workers and prominent members of the church and Sabbath school, as well as two in civil office, fell, and four of the most promising young people were taken away by death. Simon Young, the loved and respected pastor of the church, who for twenty-nine years had labored among the people, fell at his post. His daughter, Mrs. J. R.

ROSA YOUNG'S CLASS.

McCoy, who was the first to die, and two sons, Edward and John Young, the former leaving a widow and four children, all perished in the plague. Ella McCoy, a girl of brightest promise, died a week after her mother. By the deaths, the school lost five of its students, John Young, Reuben Christian, Ella McCoy, and Martha and Clarice Christian. Little Willie Christian was the only one from the younger department who died. The three others who succumbed to the dread malady were Elias Christian, father of little Willie, Childers Young, and a two-year-old baby, Emma Christian.

The present writing witnesses the visit of the *Pitcairn* on her second return trip to San Francisco. When she leaves, Elder Gates and family will leave too, also three young persons from the island will take passage on her for California, to attend school there. Miss Andre remains with us until duty calls elsewhere. With the *Pitcairn* came letters of sympathy and cheer from friends in Australia, where the news of his wife's death met Mr. McCoy.

What further awaits this little island is still in the future. Nearly two years ago, in October, 1892, when the *Champion*, man-of-war, called, Captain Rooke presided at a meeting held to inquire into the altered religious views of the people, and that something of the same nature is yet in store for the community is what is strongly believed.

Since the advent of the *Pitcairn* there have been more frequent communications between the Norfolk

Island people and their relatives on Pitcairn Island, but the means of communication with the outside world is far from satisfactory.

Several among the people of the island have taken short trips to Tahiti and Mangareva, and have returned, and in 1891 two young men went to California and Oregon, on a British bark, the *Earl Dunraven*, whose captain, a friend of the islanders, brought a large gift of clothing and many useful things from kind friends in the places he visited.

In writing this account of facts concerning Pitcairn Island it is felt that it would be unjust not to mention everyone to whom the people are indebted for favors unnumbered; but that is scarcely possible; only we feel it beyond our power to express the debt we owe to so many, and as the years come and go, and bring us to the grand close of all earthly things, we can only pray that those who have watched over us in supplying our wants may meet a rich reward.   The unceasing efforts that have been put forth by friends in the long past, and by those who have risen to fill their places, to elevate and benefit the people, have not all been in vain, and whatever of good has been accomplished, all under God, is owing to those efforts.

No account of the history of either Pitcairn or Norfolk Island—the latter in regard to the second "social experiment" carried out there, viz., the occupation of that island by the descendants of the *Bounty* mutineers—can be complete without a mention of two who figured largely in the early history of the settlement

of Pitcairn Island by the mutineers and their descendants. These two were John Buffett and the Rev. G
H. Nobbs, who, especially the latter, from the time of
their advent among the small community in 1823 and
1828 respectively, continued to do all that lay in their
power for the social benefit of the people, even though
some most serious mistakes were made.

Mr. Nobbs, who so closely identified himself with
the people, and whose constant effort was to promote
their best interests, closed his long and useful life in
November, 1884, going down to his grave respected
and honored by all, and leaving behind him sons well
qualified to sustain his honored name.

John Buffett, also, who so nobly volunteered to shut
himself off from all the fascinations that the world may
have contained for him, and chose to cast in his lot
with a community so insignificant and so remote, that
he might help John Adams in his declining days, in
the arduous duties and heavy responsibilities that the
rearing of a youthful colony necessitates, passed away
in May, 1891, having nearly completed a century of
years. He also left numerous descendants behind
him; all his children, consisting of seven sons and one
daughter, survived him, children of whom he had no
cause to be ashamed. His companion, John Evans,
who for the love that he bore him deserted his ship,
and hid himself away that he might remain with Buffett, died in December of the same year, 1891, at a
very advanced age, being tenderly and lovingly cared
for by his only surviving daughter and her children.

In this record of deaths may fitly be mentioned that of another who performed no mean part in seeking to raise the social standing of the people over whose children he was placed as their schoolmaster. Mr. Thomas Rossiter, who for many years faithfully fulfilled the heavy duties of teacher of a large school on Norfolk Island, duties for which he was eminently qualified, after some time resigned his place to others. His death occurred in 1893. The school is now conducted by Mr. Alfred Nobbs, a son of the Rev. G. H. Nobbs, assisted by a few other teachers.

A few more words concerning the great mortality attendant on the epidemic that resulted so fatally among the inhabitants of Pitcairn Island during the months of August, September, and October, 1893. With the exception of three or four of the islanders, the entire community suffered more or less from the terrible visitation. The missionaries resident on the island at the time wholly escaped the pestilence, a fact which was doubtless due to the beautiful regularity of habits that they unfailingly practiced, and the remarkable and beneficent results of which were so noticeable during the time of the fever. That the irregular habits of the people both in eating and sleeping had much to do in producing such fearful consequences there can be no doubt, and this matter, which had before been plainly presented to the people by the faithful missionaries, but which had not received the amount of attention that its importance demanded, was after the fever more strongly than ever urged upon the people, their own example serving, more than the precepts they taught, to illustrate the truth of their teachings. The result of all is that now the community that had for so long neglected the plainest principles of the laws of health, are beginning to realize that they cannot always ignore those laws with impunity, nor disregard them without great injury to themselves —a lesson that the saddest experience through which they have passed served but to deepen and impress upon their minds, minds that had hitherto been too indifferent and careless in regard to these things, and too slow to comprehend the importance of them. Every step taken in the right direction has, under God, been the result of the faithful teachings of Elder Gates and his wife, who before they left had the satisfaction of seeing a reformation in the dietary habits of the people.

The question has been frequently asked whether the people degenerate physically in consequence of too close relationship in marriage. To this the answer must be given in the negative, unless, as someone has observed, the loss of the front teeth, which is quite general, be a sign of degeneracy. But, in the writer's opinion, that is the result of not paying a more strict attention to the care and cleanliness of the teeth, and no doubt also to the fact that the food usually eaten is not of the kind to strengthen and preserve them.

The civil government of the island differs somewhat to what has been the custom for years. When the *Champion*, man-of-war, visited the island in October,

17

1892, Captain Rooke presided at a meeting convened
to consider some questions, civil and religious, acting
as regards the former agreeably to the opinion of the
British Consul at Tahiti, with whom he had consulted
when on the eve of leaving Tahiti for Pitcairn Island.

The outcome of the meeting was as follows: 1. It
was moved and carried that seven members of parliament be elected. 2. Those seven, having been elected
by general vote, will next proceed to elect from their
own numbers the next magistrate to hold office yearly.
3. It was suggested that not less than five of the seven
meet to form a quorum to consider any business—all
seven if the question be very grave.

Some other points were brought forward and discussed at some length, but it is sufficient for the purpose to mention only these. The resolutions proposed
were soon acted upon, and the plan was found to work
well. The women as well as the men have a vote.

As regards the present social standing of the people
a few words might be said. Many who have visited
the island have gone away with the impression that
the favored inhabitants breathe a purer air than other
people, and an atmosphere wholly untainted by sin;
but it is difficult to conceive how such an idea can for
a moment be entertained concerning any place upon
earth which is inhabited by any of Adam's fallen race.
Human nature is human nature the world over, and
fallen at that, so that it is certainly a mistake to think
that, because so remote from the rest of the world, no
vice or sin of any kind mars the character or degrades

the reputation of those who dwell so secluded from the world. But Satan found an entrance into the Eden home of our first parents ere yet they had known of the existence of sin, and who inheriting their tainted nature dare hope to escape his snares? Further, how was it possible that a people sprung from such a debased stock as settled the island over a century ago, and in whom runs the blood of those who stopped short at no crime, could be pure and stainless in character? A beautiful simplicity no doubt characterized the lives of the little community that grew up under the fostering care of John Adams, and, indeed, all through a century's period much of that simplicity still remains, but it is a mistake to cherish the idea that sin does not have a kingdom on the little island; and while it is cause of deep and humble thankfulness to God that He has, by His mercy and through the instrumentality of a multitude of Christian friends, kept the people from sinking into the lowest state of degradation and sin, it is also a fact to be deplored that there are among the people strong tendencies in a wrong direction, tendencies that God's grace alone can keep in check.

The visits of the missionary ship *Pitcairn* from the island of that name to Norfolk Island are hailed with unfeigned pleasure, as it is by that means that the two communities so closely related by blood have any certain communication with each other. These visits are the means by which the younger portion of the two communities have their interest in each other awakened. The dear ties that bound so closely the hearts of the older members, though sundered by distance, were never lost sight of, but it was scarcely to be expected that younger members, growing up without any knowledge of one another, should preserve undiminished the same feelings of kindred affection that their fathers and mothers possessed, and so it is matter for thankfulness that the old ties are being revived and strengthened.

APPENDIX TO FOURTH EDITION.

THE interest manifested · in that far-away mite in the Pacific—Pitcairn Island—and the avidity with which the first two editions of this book were sought for, has led the publishers to issue this improved edition.

Since the publication of the book many articles in regard to Pitcairn have appeared in the newspapers in all parts of this country.

The New York *World* sent a letter of inquiry to Miss Young, the author of this book, in October, 1893, and her answer appeared in that paper under date of January 13, 1895.

The letter is of such general interest and conveys such recent news from Pitcairn, that it is thought best to publish it herewith.

We also append an article published in *Harper's Weekly* of December 8, 1894, describing a visit made by Captain Cornelius A. Davis to Pitcairn in March, 1894. The article is of particular interest because it comes from a disinterested observer.

PUBLISHERS.

MISS YOUNG'S LETTER TO THE "SUNDAY WORLD."

PITCAIRN ISLAND, in the South Pacific, }
August 18, 1894. }

To the Sunday World—

It is probable that, such a long time having elapsed before you received any reply to your letter, you have taken it for granted that it never reached its destination. The facts in the case are that it arrived here on the 3d of February last, having been sent on from San Francisco, thence to Tahiti, and from that place to Wellington, New Zealand, to the brigantine *Pitcairn*, our missionary ship, which brought it here on the above-named date.

It should have been replied to in February, and the answer

(255)

sent you *via Pitcairn*, bound to San Francisco, which place she reached somewhere near the end of March, but having had some considerable writing then on hand which it was absolutely necessary that I should finish, I was obliged to let some of my letters go unanswered, yours among the rest, and then, in the unavoidable hurry and bustle consequent upon leave taking, it was forgotten until a day or two ago.

Please pardon my carelessness, which has been quite unintentional, as I am one who does not believe in ignoring the correspondence of anyone, and would think myself guilty of rudeness not to send a reply to anyone who should show enough interest in us and our island's history as to request any information that it is in my power to give.

I will with pleasure answer your questions, for the readers of the great *Sunday World*, and trust they may prove satisfactory to you, but, first, a fact or two concerning myself may prove of interest.

I am Young (one of the descendants of the original settlers), but young no longer in years, having completed my forty-first year five days ago, on the 13th inst. At the date when your letter was written, October 26, I had just passed the crisis of a fever typhus that had taken as victims twelve of our number, my honored and beloved father among the number, and, in addition to him, two brothers, a sister, and a niece.

In regard to the wish expressed in one or more of my published letters that you mentioned, *i. e.*, that of paying a visit sometime to the outside world, or, rather, to some portion of it, that wish remains still ungratified. My mother's father was an Englishman, who, at the age of twenty-six, decided to cast in his lot with the little handful of children of the mutineers who were in 1823 ruled over in a sort of patriarchal manner by the sole survivor of the mutineers, John Adams.

He, Adams himself, unlettered and unlearned, had, after all the rest of his companions died, most of them having been murdered, wakened up to a sense of the great responsibility that rested upon him, with the growing young community on his hands, and when, in 1823, a whale ship, the *Cynes*, hap-

pened to call in here, he expressed the earnest wish that someone would feel sympathy enough for him and the worse than
orphaned children he was striving to lead, according to the
best light he had, upward to God and good, to remain and
assist him.

My grandfather, John Buffett, remained, and ever since I can
remember his talking about his early boyhood home in Bristol,
England, it has been my wish one day to go there.   That dear
hope is abandoned.   I had a sister who married, and took her
two little boys away to Cardigan, Wales, to her husband's
home, and she passed very near our grandfather's early home,
but that was all.

Since she went away to Wales, over eight years ago, it has
been the earnestly expressed wish of my heart to pay them a
visit, but my sister died in April, 1887, having been there only
eleven months, and my earnest, longing wish to see my dear
little nephews again will never be realized.

I have had frequent invitations from many dear, valued
friends to visit America, but can see no open way yet.   I had
my trunk packed ready to go to California last year, but unfore-
seen circumstances prevented it.   Five of our people from this
island went, but I was not one, although I deeply grieved over
it.   All those who went have returned, with the exception of a
young man now at school at Healdsburg, and a charming little
girl adopted for a time by a minister and his wife, who have
been living here, a Mr. and Mrs. Gates.   I shall now take up
and answer, in regular order, the points in your letter about
which you request information.   First, school work.

How I happened to become connected with that work was
in this way—I shall have to go back many years to begin at the
start : In the years 1857-1858 two families, not being altogether satisfied with the change of living on Norfolk Island,
left that place and returned here, to their old home.   Those
families consisted of fifteen or sixteen persons, Moses Young
and family, and Mayhew Young and family, which were mostly
children by the wife's former husband, a McCoy.   It may interest you to know that Mayhew was so named for Captain May-

hew Folger, the American captain who discovered, away back
in 1808, that this island was inhabited by the children of the
mutineers.

Well, to be brief, my own father, Simon Young (I cannot
begin to tell you how good he was), feeling that the children of
the two families that first returned needed someone to look
after their educational and spiritual affairs, determined that he
would make the effort to return also and do what he could for
them. His own educational advantages had been very limited,
but he had made the very best use he could of them, and had
taught the children, while on Norfolk Island, the art, at least,
of reading, writing, and the four principal rules in arithmetic.
So, in December, 1863, our family and a few others besides
left Norfolk Island to come back here, arriving in the early part
of February, 1864.

We left a good school and teacher behind, and I have never
ceased to regret that it was never my privilege to have gone
through some regular course of study, to better enable me to
accomplish what has since been my life work, for I was only
ten when my return here was made.

As soon as possible father took up the work of teaching the
few children and young people as best he was able, and, at
about fourteen years of age, I began to help him by putting the
youngest through the alphabet and first reading lessons. I have
had no educational privileges, and only do the best I can, with
what success will be known in the great hereafter.

In February, 1893, Miss Hattie Andre, a young lady just
graduated from a college in Michigan, arrived here to take
charge of the school. My loved and honored father, sixty-nine
years of age, then retired from the work, leaving it in the hands
of Miss Andre and myself. She has a membership of about
thirty-four of the young people, and I teach twenty-one of the
youngest children, from the age of seven to fourteen, two
of mine being Dano-Spanish boys from Mangareva, one of
the Gambier Islands. Their sister attends Miss Andre's school.

You inquire about our religious belief. When John Adams
took up the work of trying to rear in righteousness the rising

young community, his sole aids to education were a Bible and
Book of Common Prayer, saved from the *Bounty*. With these
extremely limited means he taught, quite successfully, the
young folks to read, and, instituting some sort of religious
services, he very naturally had the liturgy of the Church of
England to pattern after.

This is what we had followed until October, 1886, when
we, as a body, and after ten years' searching "whether those
things were so," and battling against most unfounded and
unreasonable prejudices, joined ourselves to that church known
as the Seventh-day Adventists—seventh day because we believe in and preach the letter of the fourth commandment of
the decalogue, and Adventists because we believe in the soon
coming of our Lord and Saviour Jesus Christ in the clouds of
heaven to take his true followers to himself.

In our view of the case this is the explanation of so much
that the world at large is at present undergoing, and which
seems so mysterious to those who do not make the prophecies
of God's word their study.

You very rightfully judged that we are kept pretty well
posted by means of newspapers and friends, who now and then
touch in here on their way to different ports, in regard to what
the world is doing, but we have no regular means of correspondence. Our friends abroad take advantage of the occasional trips of our little missionary ship to send us letters and
anything else, as she always comes direct to us after leaving
California. She arrived on the 17th ult. and proposes to make
a quick return to America (if she is not sold, as has been arranged), where she will be about the end of the present year.

Several of our people have made visits to some of the neigh-
boring islands and some have gone to England and back, but I
do not think the words "dissatisfied with our lot" can be
properly applied to anyone here. In regard to myself personally, I am so in love with the free, natural life I enjoy here that
I would not willingly exchange it for any other, much as I
would enjoy a visit to your shores and to see in reality the life of
the world of which I have read so largely—life in all its phases,

from the high-toned "society" life to the very lowest. So that I do not feel that "surprised" would correctly describe my impressions.

Yes, marriage is—shall I say it?—committed among our people, the different family names numbering seven. Young, McCoy, and Christian are of the original families, and those who have come in later on are Buffett, Warren, Butler, and Coffin, the last three being Americans, and only the very last, Coffin, still lives. I think away back in the long past there were some curious "love stories" which would prove quite interesting reading, and within my own knowledge there are several that would make a good foundation for very entertaining stories should someone be found to weave them.

From the time of John Adams until the last marriage ceremony took place here—that was in 1889 (I seem to see you smile at the long space that intervenes)—the form used has been that of the Church of England. In the eighties the young people seemed to think that the chief end of man and woman, or rather of boy and girl, was marriage; and scarcely had they arrived at man's and woman's estate, certainly not to the estate of wisdom and prudence, when marriage was contracted. At present, and it gladdens my heart to see it, more efforts are made at getting some education than in getting married, and we have quite a company of young men and women who think more of getting what they can out of their schoolbooks than of being bound for life to one another.

I am not exactly posted as to the number of inhabitants here at present, but think that after the fourteen deaths that took place last year the population is about 136 only, the largest part being children under the age of sixteen.

It is quite universally accepted among people of the world outside our own little speck of earth that coined money is an almost unheard-of, unknown, and, of course, unused article among us, but such are not the real facts in the case. Our circumstances make it possible to exist, as far as the necessities of life are concerned, without the use of money, i. e., as far as food, fuel, water, and our houses are concerned, but for clothing we depend upon the product of our island, which we sell, when the opportunity offers, to a trader who calls here and brings us our supplies in that line. In addition to this, many friends have contributed from time to time very largely to our comfort in gifts of clothing and other things that we cannot procure here.

Our "standard of value" is the American dollar and the English pounds, shillings, and pence, on which no discount is made here, as we are English subjects. It would amuse you to see how many and various are the coins that pass through our hands, and whose value often puzzles us. As we are not in a postion to obtain (except on occasions when we are visited by a British ship of war) more than a few cents at a time, in exchange for fruit and curios, we do not, as do Sabbath schools abroad, contribute every week, but the dimes, quarters, shillings and pence that may be obtained from passing ships are carefully hoarded for the quarterly donation.

We have a Sabbath school of 125 members, varying in age from two years to seventy-two ; and happy the child, as well as the grown-up, who has an offering as large as a quarter to donate at the beginning of every quarter. We are glad at the thought of our little " mite " contributed towards the missionary ship *Pitcairn*, the first one to be built and used in the interests of the Seventh-day Adventists, and that our Sabbath school is self-supporting.

Our amusements consist, I may say, in a change of occupations. A peculiar way in which to amuse one's self, you will think, but really our time is too fully occupied in so many different ways to have time or inclination even for amusements that are amusements merely. If the boys can have enough powder for their guns to boom away at their own sweet will, they ask for no greater pleasure,and one unwearying source of enjoyment for the young people here is to gather around an organ and spend the time in singing to the accompaniment of the instrument.

You ask if a photographer has ever come to our shores. Yes, many of them, and many views have been taken, not only of the varied scenery, but of the people, mostly in groups. Last

March an American shipmaster, Captain Davis, was here and
spent most of his time taking pictures. Among others, he took
that of Miss Andre and her school, and of me and my bare-
footed little boys and girls.

The gentleman and lady mentioned above, Mr. and Mrs.
Gates, had been living with us for eighteen months, and last
February, when they were leaving, I gave Mr. Gates a manu
script copy of a little work I had been writing, the facts connected with this island's history from the time it was inhabited
by the *Bounty's* mutineers up to date. I did not confine myself to solid work, but only wrote at long intervals, so that what
should have been finished within a short time was dragged out
to a length of six years. Possibly some of the photographic
views taken here will be used to illustrate the little work. It
should be going through the press now, if not already gone,
and will be brought out in book form –only a very simple,
modest affair—at the Pacific Press, Oakland, Cal., where you
may obtain a copy if you have enough interest in it to order
one.

I have already written longer then I should have done, and
fear my long letter will prove a tax to your patience, but your
questions have been answered at some length, so I trust you
will excuse my trespassing on your valuable time to read all
this product of my pen.

I shall be pleased to have you write when you are so inclined,
and also to learn when you get this letter.

Yours very cordially,   ROSALIND A. YOUNG.

A VISIT TO PITCAIRN ISLAND.

WHEN Captain Cornelius A. Davis, of the five-masted
schooner *Governor Ames*—the only schooner of her class in
the world, as well as the largest fore-and-aft vessel in existence
—dropped anchor off Pitcairn Island, four thousand miles south
of San Francisco, a few months ago, he was surprised to find
himself greeted by name by a delegation of islanders who came
on board. The inhabitants of the historic little island are accus-

tomed to keep a sharp lookout for all passing vessels, and as soon as one is sighted in the offing, a boat pushes out to her, carrying friendly greetings and the offer of any assistance that may be needed. From each captain news of the ship he has left behind in the last port is obtained, together with the probable date of their sailing; so that in a majority of instances when a vessel reaches Pitcairn she is recognized immediately, and the skipper discovers that he does not need any introduction to his new-found island friends—for such they very soon prove themselves to be. He is invited to land and partake of the best the island affords, and the impression he carries away with him is uniformally a pleasant one. Captain Davis says that he would have been glad to stay at the island two or three days if there had been any good excuse for doing so, but after he had secured some fresh fruit for the crew, he felt compelled to resume his voyage. Puget Sound had been left behind thirty-five days earlier, and Liverpool was still one hundred and twenty-nine days away.

There is no more picturesque incident, perhaps, in the annals of marine venture than the mutiny on board the British ship *Bounty*, in 1789, and the subsequent landing of several of the mutineers on Pitcain Island, a speck of land which had been discovered some years before by Carteret, and named for the midshipman who first descried it from the masthead. These mutineers, fearing punishment, resolved to hide themselves from the world, and accordingly sought out this lonely spot, and, together with a number of Polynesian men and women, founded a new community far from the ordinary track of commerce. At first, according to the scant historical accounts which have come down to us, there was riot and reveling on the island, but gradually the rougher element in the population disappeared, and when the American vessel *Topaz* rediscovered the little settlement in 1808, it seems to have been orderly and prosperous. For more than half a generation the whereabouts of the mutineers of the *Bounty* had been a mystery, and their rediscovery at this time aroused a good deal of interest, especially in England. It was as if the sea had given up its dead. Everything pertaining to the little strip of land in the far Pacific was hailed with interest, and in the eighty-six years since then many books and papers descriptive of it and its people have been written. In a few weeks another volume is to be published in California by the Seventh-day Adventists, who have recently succeeded in converting the islanders to their faith. Formerly they were associated with the Church of England.

The community to-day is a model one in many respects. Since the time of the hardy mutineers a great change has taken place, and it is said that nobody on the island ever indulges in intoxicants, tobacco, or profanity. A rude church and schoolhouse—the structure shown in two of the illustrations accompanying this article—has been erected, and one of the descendants of the early settlers preaches regularly to all the members of the settlement, for church going is regarded as a matter of course on Pitcairn; and, moreover, there are not very many other divertisements. When it is remembered that there are only about one hundred and thirty people on the entire island, and that the island is scarcely three miles in length, it is easy to understand the lack of excitement which sometimes characterizes life there. And yet a spirit of intense loyalty pervades the community. Nobody has any desire to remove permanently to any other place, and those who visit the United States and Great Britain do so merely to prepare themselves for more useful labor at home. The other day young Henry Christian, a descendant of the leader of the mutiny on board the *Bounty*, arrived in San Francisco, whither he had come for the purpose of pursuing a course of study at an American school, but there can be no doubt that he will return in due time to Pitcairn. With him came also the president of the island, James R. McCoy; for the islanders elect an officer with this title, although they are under the nominal rule of England. Queen Victoria sent them two lifeboats some years ago, and these are used constantly in boarding the vessels that anchor off shore. A British flag, too, flies from one of the peaks of the island, the flagstaff being planted in the muzzle of one of the old cannon with which the *Bounty* was equipped.

Captain Davis is an expert amateur photographer, and he succeeded, during his few hours' stay on the island, in getting some admirable views of the people and their surroundings. One of these views [see page 231] shows most of the adult inhabitants grouped around Miss Andre, a young woman from Ohio, who assists the native minister in his religious work, and instructs the men and women of the community in the ordinary branches of education. Captain Davis listened to a well-recited lesson in geography the day he was there, and he says that these grown-up students seemed intelligent and eager to learn. Their faces are strong and impressive, and while there is a considerable trace of "Kanaka" blood in most of the countenances, others are thoroughly Caucasian. The mixture of totally dissimilar races has in this instance, at least, resulted in a sturdy, resourceful, and self-reliant stock.

The primary school is taught by Miss Rosa Young, a native of Pitcairn, and the author of the book descriptive of the island which is about to be published. She is the island editor as well as schoolteacher, writing a chronicle of the community from time to time, which passes from one to another of the people. There is no printing press on the island, and this is the only contemporary record of its doings enjoyed by the settlement. But then, with only one hundred and thirty people to keep track of, doubtless everybody who is so inclined contrives to be pretty well posted. On two different occasions Pitcairn has been deserted by its inhabitants, for one reason or another, and the present inhabitants are descended mostly from two families who returned to the island as late as 1858. In 1830 the eighty-seven people then resident there removed to Tahiti through fear of drought, and, though the moral laxity of the latter place so disturbed them that they went back to Pitcairn the next year, in 1856 they undertook a second pilgrimage, this time to Norfolk Island, where many of them or their descendants live to-day. William and Moses Young, together with their families, however, appear to have pined for Pitcairn, and accordingly journeyed back there again.

The landing place shown in one of the pictures [see page

27] on another page is at Bounty Bay, where the original settlers of the island destroyed their vessel more than a hundred years ago, and where, as the illustration shows, many of the inhabitants gathered to bid Captain Davis good-by. Up from this spot runs a path to the settlement itself, which is three or four hundred feet above the level of the sea. The main street is bordered with palm trees, and the thatched cottages on either side give evidence of thrift and prosperity. There are no cows or oxen on the island, but goats are plentiful, and as the land is steep and rocky in places, these sure-footed animals are doubtless better adapted to the needs of the people. Oranges grow in abundance, and so do sweet potatoes, yams, bananas, and pineapples. Captain Davis says that the dinner provided in his honor at the house of the Advent missionary was bountiful and excellent.

In these days of hurry and bustle it is refreshing to catch a glimpse of an Arcadian community like this, whose little world is far removed from all our modern tendencies in civilization. There are no telephones or telegraphs on Pitcairn Island ; no oceanic cable brings from the distant mainland the tidings of war or catastrophe on the other side of the globe. Scarcely any of the inhabitants ever saw a railway train or an electric light, and probably not even one of them has ever been inside of a theater. The papers and magazines that they read are weeks old by the time they reach Pitcairn, and much that they contain must be as unintelligible as Greek to the islanders. What do they know of college football games? or how much can they comprehend of the excitement of a presidential election? They are a people apart, and their horizon is bounded by limitless sea and sky.—*Henry Robinson Palmer, in Harper's Weekly, December 8, 1894.*

CPSIA information can be obtained
at www.ICGtesting.com
Printed in the USA
BVHW05s0311090418
512765BV00001B/2/P